Becky Excell is a full-time gluten-free food writer with a following of over 500,000 on her social media channels and 1 million monthly views on her award-winning blog. She's been eating gluten-free for over 10 years and has written recipes for numerous online publications, as well as doing cooking demos at events including the Cake and Bake Show and the BBC Good Food Show. She gave up a career working in PR and marketing to focus on food full-time, with an aim to develop recipes which reunite her and her followers with the foods they can no longer eat. She lives in Essex, UK.

BECKY EXCELL

QUICK + EASY GLUTEN FREE

Over 100 Fuss-Free Recipes for Lazy Cooking and 30-Minute Meals

Photography by Hannah Hughes

Hardie Grant

QUADRILLE

This book is dedicated to every gluten-free person who spends way more time in the kitchen than they'd otherwise like.

ABOUT
THIS BOOK

How would you sum up being gluten-free in two words? If you had asked me that back when I first had to ditch gluten over a decade ago, 'quick' and 'easy' would have been below many other (likely very unsavoury) words on my list.

Suddenly, eating at home required cooking entirely from scratch; something that wasn't easy when the supermarket seemed to drastically shrink in size overnight. Oh, and there was one other small problem: I couldn't cook or bake to save my life!

Eating out saw me limited to a tiny gluten-free menu (if I was lucky), where quite often I didn't even truly fancy any of the gluten-free options available. Worse still, on days where I didn't feel like cooking, ordering a takeaway often felt more like gambling with my health than a quick, convenient, time-saving meal.

So does all of that mean I would be stuck in this never-ending cycle of feeling 'hangry' (a convenient word to describe being simultaneously hungry and angry)? Should I just accept that all my favourite meals were off the menu for good? Well, for the first few years of being gluten-free, it certainly seemed that way.

However, it took me many years to realize this: **cooking and baking at home is the fastest way to unlock all the foods that we can't ever eat and yes, it *can* be quick and easy.** In fact, my own kitchen quickly became my favourite place to eat. But best of all, any 'muggles' (people who can eat gluten) at the table would never even notice any difference in looks or taste, so **there's no need to make dinner twice; once for yourself and again for everyone else.** That in itself is a massive time-saver!

So what's the secret to making gluten-free food quick and easy without compromise? Well, to be honest, the answer is something that simply didn't exist when I first started my gluten-free journey: having the right recipes - the kind you'll find over 100 of in this book.

Firstly, **all the recipes here in my fourth book focus on reuniting the reader with all the foods and flavours that gluten-free folks ordinarily never get to enjoy.** Because there's nothing worse than picking up a recipe book and the only things suitable for you are some form of salad, soup or fruit-based dessert, agreed?

Secondly, **each recipe comes pre-loaded with the gluten-free know-how that took me over a decade to learn.** As I discovered very soon into my gluten-free journey, using 'regular' recipes and adapting them to be suitable for a gluten-free diet can often be an exasperating task. For starters, regular recipes obviously contain ingredients we can't eat, which usually then leads to hours spent Googling 'is [insert gluten-containing product here] gluten-free?' or, 'what should I use instead of [insert gluten-containing product here]?' Fortunately, there's no need for any of that business here!

Also, blindly swapping wheat flour for a gluten-free flour blend can be a quick road to a waste of ingredients, especially when baking. And of course, both of these dilemmas can quickly become massive time-wasters.

Lastly (and this might even be the most important bit) **these recipes assume that you don't have all the time in the world** – because, let's face it, quite often we don't! First of all, you'll find that all of the products in this book are easy to source in supermarkets – no online scavenger hunt required. And, of course, these recipes are designed to get dinner on the table as soon as possible or with as little effort as possible, or in most cases, both.

All of the breakfast, lunch, fakeaways, weeknight favourites, speedy sides, party food and sweet treats chapters in this book can be made in **30 minutes or less.** Then there are two 'lazy' chapters – comfort food and lazy bakes and desserts – that require

15–20 minutes of effort, then you can put your feet up while they cook, bake or chill. Combine this with the quick cooking tips over on page 22 and you'll easily find that you can beat my estimated prep and cooking times, no problem.

Best of all, as this book contains recipes that you'd never know were gluten-free, you can happily enjoy them with muggle friends and family too. That means there's certainly no need to spend time cooking two separate meals every day!

Of course, if we're talking about making your gluten-free cooking quicker and easier, meal planning and meal prep are huge game changers too. So I would highly recommend that you use this book alongside my planner *How to Plan Anything Gluten Free*, which not only guides you through the process, but gives you heaps of space to plan out your meals each week. It also doubles up as a handy food diary, which is extremely helpful if you suspect that there may be something other than gluten that disagrees with you.

Don't forget to check out my social media channels (**@beckyexcell**) or head over to my blog **glutenfreecuppatea.co.uk** for more gluten-free recipes and inspiration too. I look forward to seeing you there!

So, if the words 'quick' and 'easy' still look strange when used in the same sentence as 'gluten-free', then I can honestly assure you that you're most definitely reading the right book.

ABOUT ME

Hi, I'm Becky and the most important thing you need to know about me is that, for many years, I struggled to adjust to a gluten-free diet. Before I make any more shocking admissions, you should probably also know that I'm a *Sunday Times* best-selling author, I've been gluten-free for over a decade and there are now 500,000 of you wonderful people following me on social media. Welcome to my fourth book, *Quick + Easy Gluten Free*.

In my muggle days (before my doctor instructed me to start a gluten-free diet over a decade ago) I relied on a gratifyingly unscheduled mix of basic cooking from scratch (often with a few convenience food products thrown in for good measure), takeaways and frequent visits to restaurants. Or, if I was lucky, my mum would throw together one of her many family favourites. Looking back, it was a carelessly chaotic harmony that I most definitely took for granted... but at the time, I simply knew it as 'normal'. However, as soon as I started my gluten-free journey, most of that went straight out of the window.

Seemingly out of nowhere, I was suddenly cooking from scratch almost every night, while at the same time trying to get my head around what I could and couldn't eat. I was a university student at the time (with all the cooking prowess you'd expect from your average student) and I can assure you that it was very far from a quick, easy or convenient transition. It felt like learning to pilot a helicopter in a hot-air balloon. In outer space.

Whenever I tried 'normal' recipes but sneakily substituted the gluten-containing ingredients with gluten-free equivalents (if they were even available), I'd often end up with wildly unpredictable results. Cooking and baking felt like I was flipping a coin that determined the fate of my poor, innocent ingredients: sometimes I'd end up with something that closely resembled what I was actually trying to make and other times I'd end up with a dry, crumbly mess that was so bad it made me laugh and cry at the same time!

When it came to using proper gluten-free recipes, out of the very few that actually worked, most would call for you to concoct your own gluten-free flour blend using flours and starches I'd never heard of – if I could even find them at all. Then there was the awkward fact that most recipe authors at the time required the use of their own unique flour blends which only worked with their specific recipes. Needless to say, it all became very confusing and time-consuming very fast. And even though I knew it wasn't true, I felt like I was the only person on Earth going through this.

It might not come as a shock to you to hear that all of the above certainly didn't help when it came to family dinners back at my mum and dad's house when I was home from university. Because, obviously, they didn't have a full arsenal of gluten-free products or their own homemade flour blends at their disposal! Plus, let's not forget that, back at the beginning, my boyfriend Mark and I were cooking two separate meals every night – one that was gluten-free, for me, and one that wasn't, for him. Now it seems so silly that we did that, but it sort of made sense at the time... even though making two meals became a huge time sponge for us.

Long story short: if I had written a recipe book during those early years of my gluten-free journey, it would have probably been called *Slow + Difficult Gluten Free*! But fortunately, this story has a happy ending.

Fast-forward 10+ years and, thankfully, a lot of things have changed for the better. These days, dinner takes around 30 minutes or less to get onto the table and, when I bake, I'm often just chatting to you guys on social media while it's in the oven. And yes, everything that comes out of my kitchen is now actually edible, just in case you were wondering!

So how did I go from one extreme to the other? First of all, the drastic expansion in the range of gluten-free products stocked in supermarkets over the last decade was a huge leap in bringing back convenience to living gluten-free. Suddenly, cooking from scratch didn't always feel quite so 'from scratch' anymore, and it remedied a lot of the time-consuming headaches that used to go hand in hand with a gluten-free diet. I no longer had to make my own gluten-free flour blends – thank goodness!

But even with a welcome explosion of gluten-free products, there was still something missing for me: reliable gluten-free recipes that were simple, quick and didn't use hard-to-source ingredients. Plus, I struggled to find recipes that focused on the foods and flavours I truly missed and craved. So, out of pure frustration, I started making my own. I began to create recipes that embraced the speed and convenience that came with all these brand new, easy-to-source gluten-free ingredients, with a generous sprinkling of everything I'd learned from cooking and baking gluten-free (almost) every day for the entirety of my twenties.

And naturally, my recipes would always be dedicated to showing you exactly how to recreate all the things that everyone in our gluten-free gang can never ordinarily eat. Perhaps best of all, because my creations didn't taste or look gluten-free, it instantly removed the need for Mark and me to eat separate meals – something that instantly saved us so much time. And since my recipes always used easy-to-source ingredients from the supermarkets, my mum was able to make my recipes in her sleep and source all the ingredients ready for whenever I came for dinner.

Having been through all of that palaver and learned everything the hard way, one thing has always been super-important to me: I never want anyone else's gluten-free journey to begin or drag on like mine did! I had zero support or knowledge, and a sparse selection of gluten-free products to work with. So if you're still feeling like you're the only person going through this, trust me, you're definitely not alone – we're all in this together! That's something I soon discovered after chatting to lots of you guys, too, so thank you from the bottom of my heart for making me realize that.

And now you know why it is my absolute pleasure to present this collection of 100+ of my quickest, easiest recipes to you, which I promise will go down well with muggles and gluten-free eaters alike. I truly hope it can make your life in the kitchen a little quicker, easier and happier and, most importantly, just make you feel normal again.

Becky x

A CRASH COURSE IN PREPARING GLUTEN-FREE FOOD

Did you know that preparing safe gluten-free food actually begins when you're still in the supermarket? It also continues when you get home and put everything away into their new homes too.

Fortunately, with a little knowledge under your belt, preparing safe gluten-free food is as quick and easy as 1, 2, 3 if you always ask yourself these three questions:

1.

Do any of the ingredients or products used have any gluten-containing ingredients or relevant allergen warnings?

First of all, triple-check the ingredients list on any products used to ensure that they don't have any gluten-containing ingredients or relevant 'may contain' allergy warnings. Here's a list of common sources of gluten that you'll need to avoid:

wheat | barley | rye | spelt
oats (see page 10 for more on oats)

Of course, even if a product doesn't have any gluten-containing ingredients, it can still be cross-contaminated through manufacturing methods.

Even naturally gluten-free products like beansprouts or hazelnuts can sometimes have 'may contain' warnings that make them unsuitable for most people who are gluten-free. I've even seen 'may contain' warnings on salt and pepper, so it's best to check everything.

I've indicated each ingredient in this book as 'gluten-free' where commonly necessary. But it's still best to triple-check the ingredients and allergy info on the packaging of every product you're using.

2.

How can I store my ingredients or products separately from gluten-containing foods?

If a gluten-free product or ingredient comes into contact with gluten at any point, it's no longer truly gluten-free. So how can you minimize that risk? Here are a few common best practices:

- Firstly, once gluten-free products are removed from their packaging, they must immediately be stored separately from gluten-containing products. This can easily be achieved by using sealed, airtight containers. It's also wise to label the containers so it's clear to everyone in the household what's inside.

- Also, remember: if you butter gluten bread, then put the knife back into the butter, the butter is no longer gluten-free. It's always a good idea to have separate butter/jam/peanut butter and condiments that are clearly labelled as being 'gluten-free only'.

3.

How can I avoid cross-contamination when preparing and cooking gluten-free food?

Carefully considering your cooking methods and any equipment used is vital in preparing gluten-free food, especially if your kitchen or utensils have previously been used to prepare gluten-containing food. So how can you minimize that risk? Here are a few more common best practices:

- Of course, gluten-free food must be cooked entirely separately from gluten-containing food.

- When deep-frying gluten-free food, do not reuse oil that has been previously used to cook gluten-containing food.

- Do not place gluten-free bread in a toaster that has been used for gluten-containing bread.

- Do not cut gluten-free bread on a board that has recently been used for gluten-containing bread.

- All utensils and surfaces must be totally cleaned down if they have previously come into contact with gluten. You can happily use washing-up liquid and dishwashers to do this.

- Ideally, you'd own utensils, pans and chopping boards that are solely dedicated to gluten-free cooking.

The moral of the story is that you can never be too careful! This isn't an exhaustive list, so definitely visit the website of your country's coeliac society for more info.

GLUTEN-FREE STORE-CUPBOARD INGREDIENTS

Meet the cast of ingredients you'll need to bring back a little normality to your gluten-free life and, most importantly, speed up your cooking or baking sessions!

These products are all easily sourced in supermarkets, either in gluten-free or 'free from' sections, but, of course, you can find them online too.

This isn't an exhaustive list of every gluten-free store-cupboard ingredient out there; just the ones I use in this book.

FLOUR

Gluten-free plain (all-purpose) flour

Unlike wheat flour, gluten-free plain flour is actually a blend of many different naturally gluten-free flours and starches; in most cases, it can be used as a substitute for wheat flour. Though it's not the 'miracle swap' some might have hoped for, it doesn't change the fact that all quick and convenient gluten-free baking (and often cooking too) relies on a reliable gluten-free flour blend, without question.

The gluten-free plain flour I use in this book can be easily found in supermarkets (I used Doves Farm's FREEE flour throughout this book) and contains a blend of rice, potato, tapioca, maize and buckwheat flour.

But as gluten-free flour is made from a blend of different flours and starches, they vary in their ratios and ingredients depending on where you live. In certain parts of the world, you might even struggle to find a gluten-free flour blend at all! That's why I've included a gluten-free plain flour blend over on page 216 for anyone struggling to find one.

Gluten-free self-raising (self-rising) flour

This all-in-one flour blend is essentially a plain (all-purpose) blend with a little added xanthan gum and raising agents too. In a quick and easy sense, a self-raising blend is super-convenient as it's essentially three ingredients in one, which will save you a little time measuring out xanthan gum and baking powder, if needed.

It's not totally uncommon to still add a little extra baking powder for good measure when baking, but for any of my pizza or quick bread recipes, self-raising flour is all you'll need. If you can't find gluten-free self-raising flour where you live, use the simple recipe on page 216 to make your own from a plain blend.

Cornflour (cornstarch)

This common white starch is priceless when you're gluten-free. For starters, as it's traditionally used to thicken sauces, you'll easily find it in supermarkets – in fact, it's one of the only naturally gluten-free starches that you can find in supermarkets. In a quick-cooking sense, a tablespoon or so mixed with a little cold water can instantly thicken any sauce, meaning you don't need to wait 20+ minutes for it to reduce and thicken. You can also use it to make XL Yorkshire puddings (page 143) or my toad in the hole on page 107, and because it's such a light starch, they puff up to be enormous!

Gram (garbanzo bean) flour

Also known as chickpea flour or besan flour, this is, not surprisingly, made from chickpeas, which of course also means that it's high in protein and has a yellow hue to it. This is actually only used in one recipe in this book where it's optional, so don't feel like you have to rush out and buy a huge bag of it. Find it in the international section in supermarkets or healthfood shops but watch out for 'may contain' warnings which can make it unsafe for coeliacs - these warnings are unfortunately quite common with gram flour.

SIMPLE SWAPS

Gluten-free oats

While oats are naturally gluten-free, unless they're labelled as 'gluten-free oats', regular oats will likely be cross-contaminated through manufacturing methods, making them unsuitable for a gluten-free diet. So they must always be clearly labelled as gluten-free!

But even still, a small number of people still struggle to tolerate oats despite them being totally gluten-free, so please be aware of that. In some countries (such as Australia), even gluten-free oats aren't considered to be suitable for a gluten-free diet. Due to both of those reasons, I've tried to minimize my use of gluten-free oats in this recipe book – purely to ensure that everyone can enjoy as many of my recipes as possible.

There's no easy like-for-like substitute for gluten-free oats, so you might just have to skip those recipes entirely if you either can't tolerate them or can't source them.

Gluten-free baking powder

Not only is this a handy ingredient that every baker should have in their gluten-free store cupboards, but I've included it here alongside an important warning: baking powder is one of those tricky ingredients that isn't actually always gluten-free. Some brands of baking powder have added wheat flour to help bulk it out or absorb water. So make sure you double-check the ingredients label of yours first to ensure it clearly states that it's gluten-free.

Gluten-free soy sauce (tamari)

You'll easily find this in supermarkets, which is very handy as most of the fakeaway recipes in this book make very good use of it. It adds an authentic umami flavour to dishes, which makes them taste like the real deal, but best of all, we can actually safely enjoy it!

Gluten-free dried pasta

Gluten-free dried pasta is a like-for-like swap that you don't really need to think twice about. However, gluten-free pasta can sometimes undesirably stick together while cooking. If that's the case, adding it straight into boiling water with a little bit of oil (and immediately stirring to separate) can greatly help reduce that effect.

I'd highly recommend giving gluten-free brown rice pasta a try too; it never sticks together and also doesn't fall apart as easily as some of the corn-based gluten-free pastas out there.

Gluten-free breadcrumbs

Here's another little time-saver that's fortunately available in gluten-free and 'free from' sections of supermarkets. Given that supermarkets are crammed with tons of breadcrumbed products that we can't eat, a small bag of gluten-free breadcrumbs can often equal endless possibilities when it comes to recreating all the foods you truly miss. Of course, you can always make your own by blitzing stale gluten-free bread in a food processor, which will reduce your food waste too.

Gluten-free stock cubes

Who could say no to a cube of instant flavour? Fortunately for us, there seems to be a wide variety of gluten-free stock cubes out there in the supermarkets at the moment. Most of them are clearly labelled as 'gluten-free', and having a good supply in the cupboard at home is never a bad thing. You can now also find gluten-free and low FODMAP stock cubes online.

Dry sherry

This is an amazing substitute for Shaoxing rice wine – a traditional Chinese wine used in lots of authentic recipes, but which ordinarily contains wheat. Dry sherry is a perfect like-for-like replacement and has a similar flavour too. You'll need this in a few of my fakeaway recipes.

Gluten-free Worcestershire sauce

Worcestershire sauce is a condiment that you can easily find a gluten-free substitute for in the supermarkets. While this is used only once in this book, you never know when you might need an instant injection of flavour.

Rice noodles

I'm sure that everyone who's gluten-free is more than familiar with rice noodles by now – that's all we're ever allowed to eat! These are naturally gluten-free and often come as either vermicelli or flat ribbon noodles. I find that dried rice noodles which also have a little tapioca starch in them to be the best by far. They have more of a bite to them and don't break anywhere near as easily when stir-frying.

Rice paper spring roll wrappers

These are commonly used in Vietnamese cooking to make summer rolls – a non-deep-fried cousin of the spring roll. They're often made purely from rice and tapioca flour, so are naturally gluten-free unless otherwise stated. These days, I often find them in the supermarket with all the Chinese-style sauces and condiments. I use them to make my gluten-free veggie spring rolls on page 157.

Gluten-free puff pastry

This ready-made pastry has been available in most supermarkets for quite a while now, but until recently the true extent of just how versatile it is somehow evaded me. I use the Jus-Rol gluten-free puff pastry, which is not only dairy-free, but vegan too – so if using other brands, please make sure you double-check if it's dairy-free or vegan first, if needed. It doesn't puff quite as dramatically as the gluten-containing version, but with the right oven timing, it can emerge quite glorious! This is an absolute essential for this book and a huge time-saver.

Gluten-free BBQ sauce

If you check the ingredients labels on your average BBQ sauce, you'll eventually find one that's gluten-free but for some reason they don't like to shout about it. It can be a real gem, as BBQ sauce isn't just for dipping; it can be used as a marinade like in my sticky BBQ ribs (page 100) or as a finishing drizzle for my hunter's chicken pasta (page 118).

BINDING

Xanthan gum

Acting as a gluten replacer, this ingredient is key to so many of my recipes working as I intended. While it comes in powder form, once hydrated it has a 'gummy' property that instantly thickens, stabilizes and binds any mixture. Though definitely nowhere near as effective as gluten, it provides all the binding we need 95% of the time.

Despite the unusual name, it's often very easy to source in supermarkets as it's such a prevalent ingredient in gluten-free baking. A little goes a long way, so generally only small amounts are called for throughout this book.

OTHER HANDY INGREDIENTS

Here are all the everyday ingredients that you'll find used throughout this book. While they should all be naturally gluten-free, it doesn't hurt to double-check the ingredients label just in case.

Eggs

Where necessary, I've indicated throughout this book whether you'll need small, medium or large eggs. It can make a big difference, especially in baking! But, did you know that a large egg in the UK is actually bigger than in the USA, Canada and Australia? Because of this, I've included a handy egg conversion guide on page 217.

Butter

While not quite as vital in this book as it was in my gluten-free baking book (*How to Bake Anything Gluten Free*), butter can be a key part in recreating so many flavours we miss. For example, it works wonders in my pan-cakes au chocolat (page 39) to create a buttery flavoured pancake with a melty chocolate middle, which somehow genuinely tastes like a real pain au chocolat pastry. Of course, it still plays a big part in some of the quick and lazy bakes in this book.

Hard margarine or hard dairy-free butter

Sometimes called a 'baking block', this is my go-to hard, dairy-free alternative to butter in baking. Unlike margarine that you'd spread on toast, this margarine comes in a hard block. It's much better at replacing butter in things like cookies or pastry, where soft, spreadable margarine just wouldn't work. Despite being a hard block, it's still softer than butter, so bear that in mind when making pastry or icing. Even if you can't find a hard block of margarine, any hard block of dairy-free 'butter' should work just fine.

Dairy-free 'buttery' margarine or spread

Thanks to the vegan revolution, the selection of dairy-free spreads and margarine is better than ever and, in most cases, you'll find it pretty easy to spot a dairy-free 'buttery' spread. This is the perfect substitution for butter when melting it or using it to fry, so I'd always recommend having a tub to hand if you can.

Dairy-free milk

Of course, if you're dairy-free, you can always substitute milk with whatever dairy-free milk you'd prefer. Results can vary depending on which type of milk you're using. For example, I usually find that pancakes often come out looking paler as a result, so bear that in mind!

Lactose-free milk

My boyfriend is lactose intolerant, so we always have lactose-free milk in the fridge. Lactose-free milk is real cow's milk, but with an enzyme called lactase added to help cancel out the lactose. Using real milk or lactose-free milk has no impact on a recipe, so feel free to use them interchangeably if you need to.

Greek yoghurt

You might be surprised to find that Greek yoghurt is a staple ingredient when I make any kind of gluten-free flatbread or pizza. It's lovely and thick and full of protein, which binds together wonderfully with a gluten-free flour blend. You can also now commonly find lactose-free Greek yoghurt in supermarkets.

Garlic-infused oil

This humble bottle of flavoured oil is used in so many recipes across this book, so please head to your supermarket's cooking oil section and pick up a bottle or two! First of all, it adds a wonderful garlic flavour to dishes without needing to take the time or effort to slice garlic and then fry it - already saving you valuable time. Secondly, if you're also intolerant to garlic like I am, then it's even more valuable. That's because, as long as it doesn't have any visible bits of garlic floating in it, garlic-infused oil is low FODMAP and suitable for those who can't tolerate garlic. This is a wonder ingredient for so many reasons! See page 18 for more info.

Black treacle

Black treacle is basically the British version of molasses. So if you can't find it readily available where you live, feel free to substitute it like-for-like if needed.

Golden syrup

This is yet another British store-cupboard staple, sometimes known as light or golden treacle. It's essentially a form of inverted sugar syrup with a distinctive, 'buttery' taste. You'll always find it with all the other syrups in the supermarket here in the UK. However, it seems to be available all across the world these days, so check the international aisle of your supermarket for it. Trust me, it's worth hunting for!

Miso paste

Mark and I have endeavoured to make all of our gluten-free Chinese fakeaway recipes as authentic as possible, but some recipes required fermented bean pastes that were either hard to source or simply weren't gluten-free. However, we discovered that miso paste did a very similar job, so we often used it instead - it's made from fermented soybeans, after all! Just make sure yours is gluten-free.

Spring onions (scallions)

In a quick and easy sense, it doesn't get any easier than spring onions. If you use the leafier, greener parts, then you can simply chop and scatter them onto your finished dishes for an instant onion flavour - no cooking required. And just like using garlic oil, it'll save you time that you'd ordinarily have to spend chopping and frying onions. Plus, if you're low FODMAP or intolerant to onions like I am, then ensure that you only eat the green parts at the top.

Minced ginger

Minced ginger is one of those magic ingredients that, again, can save you tons of time when you're cooking. Instead of buying a big hunk of fresh ginger that you never finish and have to grate or chop, you can easily buy a little jar of minced ginger. It's ready to add to your cooking - instant, no chopping required. You can usually find it with all the other spices in the supermarket.

Minced chilli paste

And the same as above goes for minced chilli paste. There's no need to spend any time at all chopping chillies or washing chopping boards when you've got a handy little jar of this. Sometimes I'll still use dried chilli flakes, but I prefer the paste when I'm making something like a curry paste or marinade where the colour of the chilli or the extra moisture is helpful.

USEFUL EQUIPMENT

These are what I'd class as the essentials for cooking and baking, assuming you have a decent set of sharp knives, pots, pans and a few baking trays already. While not everything is mandatory for this book, if you have all this, then you can basically make everything!

Fan oven

Of course, any sort of oven will do, but I mention fan here especially as this book has quick in the title! Not only does a fan oven heat up faster, but it can also reach slightly higher temperatures, which will of course cook your food more quickly, especially if you've got things cooking or baking on multiple shelves.

BAKING TINS (PANS), PIE DISHES AND ROASTING DISHES

12-hole muffin or cupcake tray

You'll need this for both of the savoury muffins in this book (pages 45 and 49) as well as the lemon and poppyseed muffins (page 165) in the sweet treats chapter. Look after yours (don't use metal utensils to ever try to prise something out of one of the holes!) and it'll last for years.

20cm (8 inch) round baking tins (pans)

This is the one thing that I assume everyone has at least one of, so if you don't, make sure you get one! It's the standard size for a sponge cake, and ideally make sure you have two for other recipes too – you can't make a sandwich cake without them.

20cm (8 inch) round loose-bottomed baking tins (pans)

Either loose-bottomed or springform baking tins are perfect for making the cheesecake in this book. I personally prefer loose-bottomed over springform as I find it much easier to get my cheesecake off of the base, but both work just as well. Also, unlike regular round baking tins of the same size, these tend to have much higher sides.

20 and 23cm (8 and 9 inch) square baking tins (pans)

The number of things you can make in a humble square baking tin never ceases to blow my mind. Plus, when you slice your creation up, you'll get perfectly square, equal slices. I use both sizes in this book.

900g (2lb) loaf tin (pan)

You'll need this for my date and walnut loaf cake on page 202, and, just as an additional handy tip: almost every loaf cake recipe you'll make in one of these tins usually qualifies as being quite a lazy bake. After all, there's no need to construct your cake – more often than not it's just one mixture that you bake and top! You don't need to break the bank for these at all either as even the cheapest options seem to be pretty durable.

23cm (9 inch) fluted, loose-bottomed tart tin (pan)

You'll need this for my chocolate cream pie on page 192, as it gives you that perfect pastry case shape despite not using pastry. Mine is also loose-bottomed, which makes removing the tart an infinitely less stressful process.

23 x 30cm (9 x 12 inch) or 23 x 33cm (9 x 13 inch) rectangular baking tin (pan)

As I have every tin under the sun (or so it suddenly seems), I use these tins quite interchangeably for traybakes and desserts, not realizing that though one has slightly higher sides, they're almost the exact same size! So definitely don't go rushing out to buy both – if you've got one or the other, it'll work just fine for any recipe that requires either dish.

18 x 28cm (7 x 11 inch) or 33 x 20cm (13 x 8 inch) roasting dish

I only own two roasting dishes and I'm not really sure I'll ever need any other sizes! I simply describe these as medium and large and you'll need both throughout this book, especially in the lazy dinners chapter.

Large, lidded and flameproof casserole dish

This is used loads in the lazy dinners chapter and is perfect in the absence of a slow cooker or pressure cooker. Mine is essentially a deep, cast-iron Dutch oven that's 23cm (9in) in diameter.

3 x 12cm (5 inch) and 1 x 20cm (8 inch) round pie dishes

For the beef and ale pie and chicken pot pies (on pages 102 and 106), you can make either one large pie, or three smaller ones using the same amount of filling and pastry. So, while again one or the other will suffice, having both will at least let you have the choice, depending on what you fancy when you're making them.

22cm (8½ inch) round bundt tin (pan)

This is a must if you want to create my chocolate doughnut celebration cake on page 198. They come in all different designs and patterns, but for this cake a less exciting bundt tin is best, or any that you feel looks more like a real doughnut! If you do have one of the more extravagant ones though, then don't worry – it'll just look like a really fancy doughnut when iced, which is certainly never a bad thing.

Ceramic ramekins

These never seem to be a uniform size, but I find that they're all around 10cm (4 inches) in diameter and anything more specific than that doesn't affect your finished bake all too much.

ESSENTIAL EQUIPMENT

Digital weighing scales

I can't emphasize how important it is to weigh out your ingredients with digital cooking scales for gluten-free baking. Amounts as little as 10 grams (⅓oz) can make a huge difference between a workable dough and a wet, sticky dough. Unlike baking with gluten, gluten-free baking has very little margin for error, so investing in digital cooking scales is always a good idea.

Rolling pin

If you intend to venture into baking gluten-free pastry, pizza dough or naan breads, then a good rolling pin will definitely be your friend. Mine comes with a variety of thickness ring guides that assist you in rolling your dough out to a specific thickness – utterly priceless!

Non-stick baking parchment

I've learned the hard way that there are definitely different grades of non-stick baking parchment. The cheapest grade still sticks and the more expensive brands are actually non-stick! So this might be an area that's worth investing in as you'll need it a lot for lining your tins, trays and pans.

Wok

For tons of the fakeaway recipes in this book, you'll need a good-quality, heavy-based, non-stick wok. It doesn't have to be the biggest in the world, but it would help! The more space you have in your wok when frying, the faster everything will cook.

Mandoline

There's no quicker or more efficient way to chop veg up to be nice and fine (so it cooks quickly) than a mandoline – no electricity required. However, please be careful and use the protective grip that comes with it as the blade is very sharp and you can most definitely cut yourself on it! Larger veg works best with a mandoline and it's very handy if you're preparing veg for frying.

Digital cooking thermometer

I can't emphasize enough how much easier your cooking life will be if you own a digital cooking thermometer. Not only can you use it to make sure meat is cooked before cutting into it, but it's great for whenever you're deep-frying food too. If you have a digital cooking thermometer, instead of guessing when the oil is hot enough, you'll know exactly how hot the oil is and when it's ready to fry (but see below, too).

Wooden spoon

You might be surprised to learn that I very rarely use a wooden spoon when I'm baking (I use a silicone spatula for that). Instead, I use my humble spoon to check the temperature of my oil for deep-frying. Simply pop the handle into the oil for 3–4 seconds – if you see bubbles gently forming around it then it's ready to fry. The wooden spoon handle test has never let me down!

ELECTRIC MIXERS AND COOKERS

Slow cooker (mine is 6.5 litres/14 pints) or pressure cooker (instant pot)

I know it might seem strange that I'd recommend a slow cooker in a book with the word 'quick' in the title, but for the lazy chapters of this book, it's priceless. All you need to do is prepare your veg and essentially just throw everything into it! So in that sense, a slow cooker can actually take up less of your time than a recipe that takes 30 minutes to make.

I've also included a pressure cooker here as for any recipe that directs you to use a slow cooker, I've provided pressure cooker timings and instructions too. In most cases, you can transform a 4-hour slow-cooker recipe into a 30-minute or less meal by using the pressure cooker. So, having one or the other is fine, but you definitely don't need both! And if you don't have either, never fear: I've also provided oven timings for all my slow-cooker recipes.

Air fryer

In case you've been living under a rock, air fryers seem to have taken the online cooking world by storm. It's basically a mini oven that not only cooks everything twice as fast, but also generally results in a crisper finish. It's not mandatory for this book, but where possible I've included air fryer timings for anyone who needs a super-speedy option. Ensure your air fryer is used for gluten-free food only in order to avoid cross-contamination (unless it's thoroughly cleaned between each use).

Stand mixer

While you can always achieve the same results as a stand mixer simply using a mixing bowl and a spatula, it'll probably take you triple the time to do so. As this recipe book doesn't contain any slightly more advanced baking, the next item is probably a little less overkill...

Electric hand whisk

I used an electric hand whisk way more than my stand mixer through the creation of the recipes in the sweet treats and lazy bakes chapters, purely because nothing required long periods of mixing. So a bit of elbow-grease-assisted electric mixing was more than enough to get the job done. If you're buying one especially, make sure it has a variety of speed settings and you're good to go.

Food processor

While a food processor isn't mandatory for this book, it can turn a 10-minute job into a 10-second job. For example, when making my veggie pakoras on page 156, if I had to slice or grate all the veg by hand using a cheese grater, I'd never get it done in under 30 minutes. But by using the grater attachment, I can shred all the veg required in a flash. It's also very handy for blitzing up biscuits for a biscuit base.

FREQUENTLY ASKED QUESTIONS

It's always good to ask questions, so sometimes I like to ask myself a few and print them here in my books. In all seriousness, these are the most common questions I get asked about my books and my recipes and they're all very relevant to the recipes in this book. So here they are...

Are there dairy-free recipes in this book?

Yes – tons, actually! Throughout the book, I've clearly labelled whenever a recipe is dairy-free. Whenever a recipe isn't dairy-free, I've listed exactly how to make it dairy-free (if possible) for each recipe. Ninety per cent of the recipes in the book are either dairy-free, or can be adapted to be dairy-free using a few simple swaps.

Are there vegetarian or vegan options?

Yes! I've clearly labelled whenever a recipe is suitable for vegetarians or vegans. If it isn't veggie/vegan to start with, I've also included instructions on how to adapt it, if possible. If I haven't provided instructions on how to make a particular recipe veggie or vegan, it doesn't mean it's impossible, it usually means I haven't had a chance to test alternative products myself. So feel free to ask in my Facebook group for further advice on adapting any recipes you fancy to be vegetarian or vegan.

I can't tolerate garlic, can I still cook your recipes?

When I tell people that there's no actual onion or garlic in my first recipe book, they can be a bit puzzled by the frequent use of garlic-infused oil - especially when they're intolerant to garlic like I am.

So here's the explanation of why garlic-infused oil is still safe for those intolerant to garlic, or on a low FODMAP diet: despite garlic oil having been made using actual garlic, the parts of garlic we're intolerant to cannot transfer into oil. They can transfer into water, which is why picking bits of garlic out of your food isn't a good idea, but in oil, it's a different matter. So in short, while the end result tastes like garlic, it is totally safe to consume for garlic dodgers. Just make sure the oil is totally clear and doesn't have visible bits of garlic floating in it, because that's most definitely not safe!

Garlic is used occasionally as an ingredient in this book, but the FODMAP key will advise you what to substitute it with - the same goes for onion too.

I can't tolerate onion, can I still cook with spring onion or leek?

Yes! This took me years to discover, but the green parts of spring onion (scallion) and leek can often be tolerated well by most people who would otherwise experience symptoms from eating onions. So, with that in mind, you'll find that I make good use of that throughout all the recipes in this book!

However, the whiter parts of spring onions and leeks are not suitable for those who are on the low FODMAP diet or intolerant to onions, so please avoid those if needed.

Are these recipes healthy? Can I make them healthier?

Some people automatically assume that anything gluten-free is healthy and are very confused by my books. So I'll get this out of the way now: not everything that's gluten-free is automatically healthy.

This book focuses on quick and easy gluten-free cooking/baking that shows you how to recreate (as closely as possible) all the foods that we always miss out on. And so often, the foods we literally never get to eat are fried, battered, breadcrumbed, as well as the obvious meat pies and bakery-style pasties, sweet treats, cakes and desserts.

Obviously, some of these things don't fit into most people's black-and-white understanding of the word 'healthy' (my opinion is 'everything in moderation' in case you were wondering). But please remember: my aim is to recreate all the foods we can't eat to be as close to the real deal as possible; after all, many of us have gone many years without enjoying them.

However, with a little know-how, you can happily make any of my recipes healthier if you fancy, so here are a few general tips:

- Whenever a recipe asks for shallow-fried, crispy-coated chicken or pork etc., feel free to just fry it without the coating in a couple of sprays of low cal cooking spray until cooked through. Then just chuck it into the sauce once it's done for an even quicker, lighter option.

- Use the air fryer cooking instructions where specified. When making coated chicken or pork or anything breadcrumbed, don't be fooled into thinking you can use zero oil at all just because it's an air fryer. Not only will it not colour without any oil, but it'll also never turn crispy; so make sure you've got a good spray bottle of oil to hand and don't be too stingy with it.

- Use a little less oil than specified or use a low cal cooking spray instead for all forms of light frying.

- Use anywhere up to a third less cheese than specified whenever a recipe calls for it. If the cheese is just used as a topping, feel free to reduce more drastically, or omit entirely.

- Feel free to reduce the sugar a little in savoury dishes, but be wary of reducing it too much whenever you also see any sort of vinegar in the recipe. Often, the sugar is there to create a sweet-and-sour flavour with the vinegar, so what happens if you reduce the sugar too much? It becomes too sour!

- When it comes to sweet treats, cakes and desserts, just have a smaller slice or portion. Messing with these recipes is always an experiment that I wouldn't overly recommend. Slicing cakes or cookies, then freezing them and defrosting individual portions, is a great way to help with portion control.

- Use light coconut milk or low-fat cream cheese instead of full-fat versions. Light coconut milk can often result in a very thin curry, but fortunately you'll notice that I've usually added a little flour to help thicken the sauce, so it should be fine. The only exception to the low-fat cream cheese substitution is in a cheesecake – I wouldn't recommend using low-fat cream cheese for it unless you're going rogue and making it in individual pots. Low-fat cream cheese simply doesn't have a high enough fat content to set and hold!

Of course, this isn't an exhaustive list, but I just really wanted to highlight how very easy it can be to make any recipe healthier and, hopefully, give you a little inspiration on how you can tweak these recipes to suit your own needs.

Can I freeze this?

You tell me! I've added this little symbol ❄ to each recipe indicating whether a recipe can be frozen or not. Defrosting times will definitely vary, but generally, the best and safest option is to defrost in the fridge overnight.

And, where possible, freeze everything separately in individual airtight containers if you can. For example, it's always a good idea to freeze battered chicken, sauce and rice separately. That way, once defrosted, you can reheat the rice and sauce separately in the microwave without the rice becoming soggy, and reheat the battered chicken in the oven or air fryer so it's still nice and crispy.

What can I use instead of xanthan gum? Can I leave it out?

We're very lucky to have xanthan gum as an ingredient when it comes to gluten-free baking – it mimics gluten (to an extent), helping to bind mixtures so they don't crumble once they're baked.

So my advice to you is: if you can tolerate xanthan gum, then please source it and use it! You can find it in every single 'free from' aisle or gluten-free section, usually next to the gluten-free flour, so it's fortunately very easy to source. Plus, I've tested and created all my recipes using it, so I can guarantee the results you'll get with it.

If you want your recipes to be entirely free of xanthan gum, I absolutely cannot guarantee results. From my experience, using zero xanthan gum makes cakes and biscuits very crumbly, bread can be brittle and pastry can be difficult, if not impossible, to work with.

Where can I buy gluten-free gram/chickpea/besan/ garbanzo bean flour?

First of all, yes, despite having all these different names, these flours are all the same thing! Most supermarket-stocked gram flour has a nasty 'may contain gluten' warning which makes it unsuitable for coeliacs.

If you can't find any without this warning, healthfood shops or online retailers are the next best port of call and, ideally, aim to buy a brand of gram flour that you recognize as being from a known gluten-free brand. If buying online, this will ensure there aren't any unwanted 'may contain' surprises because they 'conveniently' forgot to mention it in the listing. As finding this product can be a tricky one, there's only one recipe which calls for it in this book (the veggie pakoras on page 156), which, fortunately, can also be made using gluten-free plain (all-purpose) flour instead.

HOW TO BE A QUICK COOK

I'll take this opportunity to re-emphasize that this book doesn't assume you have advanced cooking or baking skills at all. But that doesn't change the fact that practice makes perfect and a little knowledge goes a long way! So here are a few tips that I guarantee will reduce the time you spend in the kitchen.

I should probably also say that these tips are by no means mandatory for this book, but if you're new to cooking, they will most definitely help to speed up your cooking sessions and hit the estimated prep and cooking times for each recipe.

1.

Prep veg and measure out your ingredients in advance

If there's measuring required, please make sure you get everything weighed out before you start. I know this seems like a self-explanatory tip, but the process of doing this makes so much difference to efficient cooking and baking that it even has its own fancy French name: *mise en place*.

For example, you'll likely notice that in the ingredients section of each recipe, not only will it list what you'll need, but it will also specify how to prepare it – such as 'red pepper, chopped into bite-sized chunks'. So here's a polite but firm reminder to get that prep done before you actually start cooking.

With all the measuring and prep done ahead of time, all you've got left is to just throw everything together in stages, something which instantly makes cooking or baking an infinitely more enjoyable process. Plus, you'll be ready for each stage of the recipe way before you even get to it.

You also get bonus points from me if you get all the cooking equipment required ready ahead of time.

2.

Use a large, sharp knife for any meat and veg chopping

I used to be the world's slowest chopper because I always used a small paring knife to chop everything... mainly because at the time it seemed the least intimidating knife! However, while it's great for more fiddly tasks, it just doesn't have enough weight behind it to efficiently get through your average meat and veg chopping task. Plus, you end up having to use quite a bit of force to even get through something as simple as a raw carrot, making the whole process a bit of a slog.

Compare that experience to using your average 7-inch chef's knife and, honestly, the difference is like night and day. It has the weight to get through even the chunkiest veg with very little force and, if nice and sharp, can slice any meat super-fast too – no sawing or hacking required. It also allows you to have more control, enabling you to cut thinner slices, which of course will then cook much more quickly and save even more time.

I can't emphasize enough how much safer a sharp knife is, especially after using a very blunt one during a cooking demo in front of a big crowd. With a blunt knife, you're so much more likely to slip which, combined with the fact that you have to put so much more force into cutting through anything, is a recipe for a very unfortunate accident!

3.

A little multitasking goes a long way

Just to clarify, we're not talking about the kind of multitasking that gives you a stress-induced headache here. I'm more referring to being smart and prepping veg or measuring out ingredients while your oil is heating. Or ensuring that you begin making that sauce while you wait for your pasta to boil. Or, simply preparing any finishing touches while your bake is still in the oven. Fortunately, all of my recipes are structured and written to encourage this, but it never hurts to have a little reminder, does it?

4.

Keep your kitchen efficiently organized

It wasn't until I wrote this book that I realized how much I either need to better organize my spice cupboard or, more drastically, get a spice rack where everything is easily visible and accessible. Why? Because I often spend so much time hunting for a particular spice that minutes pass before I even find it.

The same ethos applies to the rest of your kitchen too! If everything is easily to hand and, more importantly, you know where it lives, then trust me, you will definitely reap the rewards of your organization when cooking or baking.

5.

Don't crowd your wok or frying pan when frying

It's simple really, but I'll say it anyway: the more food you have in your pan at once, the longer it'll take to cook. In fact, if you overload your wok or frying pan, your food will tend to sweat instead of fry, resulting in more of a soggy finish while also taking longer to cook, which is definitely not what we're going for here. The best solution to this is having a large wok and at least one large frying pan.

Bigger pans are especially handy when making pancakes or shallow-frying; the larger surface area simply allows you to fry more at once, meaning you can often fry everything in two batches instead of four – effectively halving the cooking time. And bear in mind that my wok and frying pans certainly aren't anything out of the ordinary in terms of size. However, I mention this here because there are smaller, more compact versions of woks and frying pans available which are, in my opinion, more suited to cooking individual meals for one, or one or two ingredients at a time.

6.

Make use of pre-prepared frozen veg

These days, the frozen veg section of supermarkets is so much more than just bags of frozen peas and sweetcorn! You'll find almost every different type of veg under the sun (or more accurately, in the freezers) and of course, they're all pre-chopped, saving you tons of prep time.

And fortunately for us, the packaging will often have instructions on how to cook them straight from frozen, either in the microwave or on the hob. Then, simply drain and chuck them straight into your pan when a recipe calls for them; just bear in mind that, as they're now cooked, they likely won't need cooking for as long as if they were completely raw. If using a slow cooker or pressure cooker for some of my recipes in the lazy chapter, you can also happily use frozen veg as if they were raw too. Speaking of which...

7.

There's nothing at all wrong with microwaving raw or frozen veg

For starters, even though the cooking time may be very similar to boiling it, by using the microwave you've completely eliminated the need to boil a kettle, pour it into a pan and then bring it to the boil again. That's already 5 minutes saved! Commonly, all you need to do is put the veg into a small dish, add a few tablespoons of water, cover and microwave on full power until cooked to your liking.

But even despite the time-saving advantages, many of us are still a little sceptical about microwaving certain foods, when we shouldn't be. Why? Well, the best way to ensure that vegetables don't lose all their nutrients during the cooking process is to cook them using the method that's as fast as possible. That way, the nutrients don't get much of a chance to escape from the veg itself. And, news flash: the microwave is actually the fastest way to get them cooked. So if you see instructions on how to prep your veg in a microwave, then please don't be alarmed and, more importantly, make sure you give it a try!

8.

Meal planning is your friend

While we're talking about being quick and efficient in the kitchen, planning your meals ahead of time using a meal planner is always a good idea. Not only will it mean you have all of the ingredients required in your fridge and cupboards already but it also means you'll have the exact recipe you intend to use pre-decided and it can also save you money while reducing the likelihood of impulse takeaway orders.

If all of the above sounds good to you, then make sure you check out my dedicated gluten-free meal planner *How to Plan Anything Gluten Free*, which has all the advice and info you'll need to get started, as well as ample space to create your own meal plans.

9.

When baking, don't forget you can always 'lazy line' your baking tins (pans)

While I'd always encourage greasing your tins and lining them before filling with lovely cake batter or whatever it is you're baking, there is a little hack I do to save a precious minute or so.

For example, when lining a 900g (2lb) loaf tin (pan), instead of greasing it, I'll often line it with paper, then use pegs or bulldog clips to hold it in place. Then, once I've filled it with my cake batter, all you have to do is simply remove the pegs or clips before you bake it. This also works really well with my traybake recipes or any recipe that calls for a square baking tin.

10.

Get a digital food thermometer

Though I praise them enough in the useful equipment section (page 16), there's no denying that one of these inexpensive gadgets can save you so much time. It instantly answers the question, 'Is my oil hot enough to shallow-fry?' or, 'is my chicken cooked yet?' by telling you the exact temperature with a quick poke of the temperature probe. Ever since I got mine, I now can't live without it and I'm thankful for all the time it saves me that I'd otherwise spend wondering if things are ready/done or not.

EASY MEAL IDEAS

Now, I don't want this section to sound patronizing or seem like a huge waste of a page, because that honestly wasn't my intention! While there are loads of recipes in this book that you can make in anywhere from 15–30 minutes for breakfast, lunch, dinner or dessert, it's all too easy to forget about these unsung heroes.

In fact, they're so simplistic and easy that they don't even need a written recipe; something which sadly works against them in a way, as they often then get forgotten about. So, consider this page a little reminder that they exist! And, of course, who could forget the fact that they're all very easily gluten-free?

BREAKFAST

- Gluten-free cereal with yoghurt or milk, topped with berries, nuts and seeds

- Gluten-free porridge spiced with a pinch of cinnamon and sweetened with a little honey, then topped with berries, nuts and seeds

- Smashed avocado on gluten-free toast, topped with toasted pumpkin seeds and a pinch of dried chilli flakes

- Soft-boiled egg and gluten-free soldiers

- Scrambled egg topped with ham or smoked salmon, served on a toasted gluten-free bagel

LUNCH

- Baked potato with cheese and beans, tuna mayo or gluten-free coronation chicken

- Canned soup and toasted, buttered gluten-free ciabatta rolls

- Salads done right with generous amounts of protein, gluten-free croutons and a gluten-free dressing, placed in a large mixing bowl and covered, then shaken about rather violently. Trust me, it's so much better when the dressing covers everything!

- Cheese on gluten-free toast with a little gluten-free Worcestershire sauce

- Leftover portions from last night's dinner, reheated until piping hot

DINNER

- Ham, fried egg and crispy oven chips with lots of ketchup

- Frozen gluten-free chicken nuggets, fish fingers or scampi with oven chips and peas or sweetcorn

- Mince and gravy... my uncle Neil's favourite! Simply cook onion and beef mince (omit the onion if you can't tolerate it) cover with gluten-free gravy and serve alongside mashed potato and steamed veggies

- Gluten-free pasta coated in pesto, served with a generous handful of rocket (arugula) and a grating of Parmesan

- Omelette using any leftovers lurking in your fridge, served with ketchup or gluten-free brown sauce

DESSERT

- Ice cream (ensure gluten-free if it's particularly adventurous in flavour) or lemon, raspberry or mango sorbet

- Ready-to-eat strawberry jelly (jello) served with cold custard

- Hot rice pudding with big dollops of jam

- Eton mess with sliced strawberries, raspberries, broken up store-bought meringue, whipped cream and a generous drizzle from a bottle of raspberry or strawberry coulis

- Stewed apple and gluten-free custard

PS: if you do actually want a recipe for any of the above – just message me!

KEY

Just as a handy reminder for those still in disbelief: **yes, everything in this entire book is gluten-free!**

But it's also incredibly important to me that as many people can enjoy my recipes as possible. That's why I've labelled all of my recipes to clearly indicate whether they're dairy-free, lactose-free, low lactose, vegetarian, vegan or low FODMAP.

But even if a recipe isn't naturally suitable for all dietary requirements, watch out for the helpful notes by the key. These will indicate any simple swaps you can do in order to adapt the recipe to your dietary requirements, if possible.

Here's a breakdown of what labels I'll be using so you know what they look like and exactly what I mean when I use them.

DAIRY-FREE

This indicates that a recipe contains zero dairy products. Ensure that no ingredients used have a 'may contain' warning for traces of dairy and double-check that everything used is 100% dairy-free. Of course, if a recipe calls for any convenience products such as gluten-free puff pastry, ensure they're dairy-free too.

LACTOSE-FREE

Lactose-free? Isn't that the same dairy-free? No, it definitely isn't! For example, lactose-free milk is real cow's milk with the lactase enzyme added, so while it's definitely not dairy-free, it is suitable for those with a lactose intolerance. The lactose-free label indicates that a recipe is naturally lactose-free or uses lactose-free products. If a recipe calls for any convenience products such as gluten-free puff pastry, ensure they are lactose-free too.

LOW LACTOSE

Butter is an integral ingredient in cooking and baking that is also incredibly low in lactose. That means that people with a lactose intolerance will have no problems tolerating it. The same goes for a lot of hard cheeses like Cheddar and Parmesan. So for those ingredients, you won't necessarily need a special 'lactose-free' equivalent. Of course, recipes that use these ingredients aren't technically lactose-free, so they'll be labelled as low-lactose for clarity. If a recipe calls for any convenience products such as gluten-free puff pastry, ensure they're lactose-free or low lactose too.

VEGETARIAN

This indicates that a recipe is both meat-free and fish-free. Where possible, I've provided simple veggie swaps where necessary and possible – just look for the key at the top of each recipe for advice. Please make sure any products and ingredients used are vegetarian-friendly.

VEGAN

This indicates that a recipe contains no ingredients that are derived from animals. Even if a recipe isn't vegan to start with, look out for the notes next to the key at the top of each recipe for advice. While gluten-free cooking and baking is a different kettle of fish from vegan cooking and baking, if it is easy to make the recipe using vegan alternatives, I'll tell you how in that section. Make sure all products and ingredients used are vegan-friendly.

LOW FODMAP

This indicates that one serving of the finished recipe is low FODMAP. The low FODMAP diet was specifically created by Monash University in order to help relieve the symptoms of IBS in sufferers. Brief disclaimer: you should always start the low FODMAP diet in consultation with your dietician. Please ensure that any convenience products you use are low FODMAP.

Here are a few quick side notes: whenever I mention spring onions (scallions) or leeks in this book, I mean the green parts only for FODMAP reasons. Also, garlic-infused oil is low FODMAP too, as long as it's clear and doesn't have visible bits of garlic floating in it.

BREAKFAST + BRUNCH

While the eternal cycle of cereal and milk is certainly quick and convenient (and, of course, can be actually very enjoyable if you find a good gluten-free cereal), there's no denying that a little cycle-busting breakfast can go a long way.

So here's a selection of my favourite speedy and convenient breakfast and brunch recipes that can all be made in <u>30 minutes or less</u>. In fact, for the recipes that take the full 30 minutes, for at least half of that time you don't even have to be in the kitchen!

So please do enjoy a selection of everything from pancakes to crêpes, waffles and microwave 'baked' oats, to baklava granola, breakfast muffins, cinnamon roll French toast, and more.

use dairy-free milk

 use lactose-free milk

 use lactose-free milk and one medium egg instead of the banana. Serve with no more than ⅓ ripe banana per person

 use dairy-free milk

- 150g (1 cup plus 2 tbsp) gluten-free plain (all-purpose) flour
- 3 tbsp light brown sugar
- 3 tsp gluten-free baking powder
- 300ml (1¼ cups) milk
- 1 very ripe banana, ½ mashed and ½ sliced, to serve
- 6 tbsp smooth peanut butter, plus an extra 4 tbsp (optional), to serve
- 2 tsp vanilla extract
- 4 tbsp raspberry or strawberry jam (jelly)
- Vegetable oil, for brushing (optional)
- Maple syrup, to serve

ELVIS WAFFLES

Serves 2 (makes 4–5 large waffles) ❄
Prep + Cook 20 mins

Though I very much doubt Elvis was gluten-free, I still 'can't help falling in love' with his famous flavour combo of peanut butter, banana and jam. It's fruity, nutty and sweet, all packed into a crispy waffle with a fluffy middle; he often enjoyed this combo with crispy bacon too, which I would highly recommend trying if you've had a tough week and are subsequently feeling 'all shook up'.

1 In a large mixing bowl, combine the flour, sugar and baking powder. In a large jug (pitcher), beat together the milk, mashed banana, peanut butter and vanilla extract until smooth.

2 Create a well in the flour mixture and pour in the wet mixture, whisking until smooth. Allow the batter to rest for 5-10 minutes.

3 While the batter is resting, mix the jam with 2 teaspoons of water in a small dish, then set aside. Next, start heating up your waffle maker. All waffle makers vary, so it's best to follow the instructions of your machine. If it requests that you brush a little vegetable oil onto it first, make sure you do this once it's heated.

4 Once the waffle maker has heated, pour in one measure of your batter – I add about 60ml (2fl oz) batter at a time, using a ¼ measuring cup. Close the lid and cook until consistently golden on the outside and a little crispy – in my waffle maker this takes 3-4 minutes. Remove from the waffle maker and keep warm in a low oven while you cook the remaining batter.

5 Serve with the sliced banana, then drizzle the jam mixture over the top. Optionally, warm up the peanut butter in the microwave then drizzle that on too. Lastly, serve with as much maple syrup as you like.

TIP The riper your banana is, the easier it will be to mash and, most importantly, the better your waffles will taste!

use dairy-free milk and yoghurt

 use lactose-free milk and yoghurt

 use lactose-free milk and yoghurt, use maple syrup instead of honey and use no more than ⅓ of a ripe banana

 use dairy-free milk and yoghurt, replace the egg with ½ ripe banana, mashed, and use maple syrup instead of honey

---

For the base

- 3 tbsp gluten-free oats
- 3 tbsp milk
- 1 tbsp natural or Greek yoghurt
- ½ tsp ground cinnamon, plus extra to serve
- 1 medium egg

For bursting blueberry oats

- Small handful of blueberries, plus extra to scatter on top
- 1 tbsp honey
- 1 tsp blueberry jam (jelly), plus extra to serve

For peanut butter and jam oats

- Small handful of raspberries, plus extra to scatter on top
- 1 tbsp raspberry jam (jelly), plus extra to serve
- 1 tsp peanut butter

For maple banana oats

- ½ small ripe banana, sliced, plus extra to scatter on top
- 1 tbsp maple syrup, plus extra to serve
- 1 tsp peanut butter

DIY MICROWAVE 'BAKED' OATS

Serves 1

Prep + Cook 5 mins

Did you know you can make baked oats in a mug or small bowl in the microwave? (Let's not debate right now about how something can be baked if it's microwaved...). It's about five times as fast and still tastes absolutely out of this world. I've included three variations that keep me happy throughout the week, but absolutely feel free to use the measurements below as inspiration to concoct your own flavour combinations.

1 Put all the base ingredients with your choice of added ingredients in a medium-sized mug or a small bowl. Beat together with a fork until smooth, with the mixture ideally filling up no more than half of your mug or bowl. Top with the extra berries or banana, depending on which variation you're making.

2 Cover the mug or bowl with cling film (plastic wrap) and pop into the microwave for 2 minutes on full power (in a 900W microwave). Allow to cool for a few minutes, then top with a little dusting of cinnamon, more jam or maple syrup.

TIP This recipe contains gluten-free oats – check page 10 for more info if you can't get hold of them.

swap the pistachios for another small handful of walnuts and use maple syrup instead of honey

use maple syrup instead of honey

- 150ml (⅝ cup) honey, plus 1 tbsp for the nuts
- 1½ tsp ground cinnamon, plus a pinch for the nuts
- ½ tsp ground cloves
- 1 tsp orange extract
- 50ml (3 tbsp plus 1 tsp) olive oil
- 250g (2½ cups) gluten-free oats
- Pinch of salt
- 3 tbsp pistachios, shelled and roughly chopped
- Small handful of walnuts, roughly chopped
- 3 tbsp roasted hazelnuts, roughly chopped

BAKLAVA GRANOLA

Makes 500g (1lb 2oz) or 10–12 servings
Prep + Cook 20 mins

This recipe is dedicated to every gluten-free person who misses baklava, which I'm assuming is everyone reading this page. With a warming orange flavour and a sweet, nutty, crunchy finish, this is a reunion of flavour in a bowl. Serve with milk or a thick, creamy natural yoghurt and thank me later.

1 Preheat your oven to 170°C fan / 190°C / 375°F and line two baking trays with non-stick baking parchment.

2 Grab a large mixing bowl and add the honey, cinnamon, ground cloves, orange extract and oil. Mix until well combined. Next, add the oats and salt and give it all a good stir until everything is evenly mixed and coated. Divide the mixture equally between the two baking trays, scraping the mixing bowl so no oats remain in it, then spread it out, leaving a few clumps of oats here and there. Bake for 7–8 minutes.

3 Tip the chopped nuts into the bowl you used earlier, add 1 tablespoon of honey and a pinch of cinnamon, then stir to mix.

4 Divide the nuts between each tray and mix in well before returning to the oven for another 8–10 minutes. The oats should all be lovely and golden brown.

5 Once cool, pop into an airtight container and store for up to a month. Enjoy with natural yoghurt or milk.

TIP This recipe contains gluten-free oats - check page 10 for more info if you can't get hold of them.

use dairy-free 'buttery' margarine and dairy-free milk

 use lactose-free milk

 use lactose-free milk

 use a hard dairy-free alternative to butter and dairy-free milk; replace the eggs with 1 tbsp flaxseed, then allow the milk mixture to rest for 10 minutes

---

- 2 tbsp butter, melted, plus extra for frying
- 3 tbsp light brown sugar
- 2 tbsp ground cinnamon
- 4 slices of gluten-free bread
- 75ml (5 tbsp) milk
- 2 medium eggs
- 2 tsp vanilla extract
- Icing (confectioners') sugar, for dusting
- Maple syrup, to serve

CINNAMON ROLL FRENCH TOAST

Serves 2

Prep + Cook 15 mins

You wouldn't believe how easy it is to work all the flavours we miss into places you might never expect. In this case, two slices of golden French toast conceal a sticky, gooey, caramelized cinnamon filling – the exact same filling that you'll find in a cinnamon roll. Trust me, this recipe needs to be on your 'must try' list!

1 Grab a small bowl and add the melted butter, sugar and cinnamon, then mix until combined.

2 Spread the butter mixture over 2 of the bread slices and top with the remaining bread to make 2 sandwiches.

3 Add the milk, eggs and vanilla extract to a large, shallow bowl. Beat with a fork until smooth.

4 Dunk your sandwiches into the egg and milk mixture until both sides are as soggy as possible. Don't forget the edges of the sandwich too! Allow them both to soak in the mixture for a few minutes, if possible.

5 Heat a little butter in a large frying pan over a medium heat. Once the butter has melted, add both sandwiches and fry on each side for 2–3 minutes, or until golden brown.

6 Remove from the pan and transfer to serving plates. To finish, dust with icing sugar and serve with maple syrup. Or, alternatively, mix 2 tablespoons of icing sugar with 1 teaspoon of water to create a glacé icing, then drizzle over the top.

use dairy-free milk and use oil to fry

 use lactose-free milk

- 110g (¾ cup plus 1½ tbsp) gluten-free plain (all-purpose) flour
- 2 tbsp light brown sugar
- 1½ tsp ground cinnamon, plus extra to serve
- 2 medium eggs
- 230ml (1 cup minus 1 tbsp) milk
- 6 tsp butter or vegetable oil
- 2 Braeburn or Pink Lady apples
- Maple syrup, to serve

DUTCH-STYLE APPLE PANCAKES

Serves 3 (makes 6)
Prep + Cook 20 mins

Each time Mark and I visit Amsterdam, we order two of these from our favourite gluten-free pancake restaurant without fail. It's essentially a cinnamon crêpe embedded with thin slices of soft, fresh apple. Serve with maple syrup and I promise you that it tastes just like apple pie. Wearing clogs while making this is entirely optional.

1 Put the flour, sugar and cinnamon into a large mixing bowl and stir to combine. Add the eggs and half the milk and whisk until smooth. Add the rest of the milk and whisk again until smooth and the consistency of thin cream.

2 Place a 30cm (12in) frying pan or crêpe pan over a low-medium heat. Add 1 teaspoon of butter or oil and tilt the pan so it covers the base of the pan as much as possible.

3 Prepare the apples by cutting them into slices 3mm (⅛in) thick, using a large sharp knife or mandoline, cutting any larger pieces in half. Any thicker than this and they will still have a little too much bite to them once cooked.

4 Arrange 5–6 slices of apple in the pan, leaving even gaps between them, then pour or spoon in enough pancake batter to almost completely cover the base of the pan. Lift the pan and tilt it to spread the mixture to completely cover the base of the pan - it should be level with your apple slices.

5 Fry for 1½–2 minutes, then carefully flip and fry on the other side for 1 minute. Slide out of the pan onto a plate and repeat using the rest of your apples, batter and butter or oil.

6 Lightly sprinkle with a little more cinnamon, drench in maple syrup and enjoy. At the restaurant we visit, you can also order this with crispy bacon on top!

TIP The pancakes will be a little delicate around the slices of apple, so be sure to not place them too close together in the pan, and be careful when you flip them!

use dairy-free 'buttery' margarine, milk and chocolate chips

 use lactose-free milk and chocolate chips

 use lactose-free milk and chocolate chips

use dairy-free 'buttery' margarine, milk and chocolate chips, and use a flax egg instead of the egg (see TIP on page 168)

- 200g (1½ cups) gluten-free self-raising (self-rising) flour
- 1 tsp gluten-free baking powder
- 260ml (1 cup plus 1½ tbsp) milk
- 1 medium egg
- 2 tsp vanilla extract
- 1 tbsp butter, melted, plus extra for frying
- 70g (2½oz) dark (bittersweet) chocolate chips
- Maple syrup, to serve

PAN-CAKES AU CHOCOLAT

Serves 3 (makes 12) ❄
Prep + Cook 20 mins

See what I did with the name there? I'm super-proud of this one because not only did I completely pull this idea out of thin air, but they genuinely taste like a pain au chocolat. By adding melted butter and golden syrup to the batter, then frying them in butter, these pancakes (not surprisingly) have a wonderful rich, buttery flavour. With a melty chocolate centre to seal the deal, this simple recipe will satisfy all your chocolate pastry cravings!

1 In a large mixing bowl, combine the flour and baking powder. In a jug (pitcher), beat together the milk, egg, vanilla extract and melted butter until smooth.

2 Create a well in the flour mixture, then pour in the liquid mixture, whisking thoroughly.

3 After 30 seconds of whisking, the consistency should be smooth, like thick cream. Allow the batter to rest for 5 minutes.

4 Heat 1 tablespoon of butter in a large frying pan over a low-medium heat. Tilt the pan to cover the entire base or use a brush to spread the butter over the base of the pan. Pour in the batter – I add about 60ml (2fl oz) at a time, using a ¼ measuring cup. You should be able to fry four pancakes in the pan at once, if your pan is large enough.

5 Immediately place about 1 teaspoon of dark chocolate chips in the centre of each pancake. Fry for 1–2 minutes until the edges are starting to look done, then flip and cook for a further 30 seconds. Don't fry for too long after flipping or the chocolate can burn!

6 Repeat with the remaining mixture. Stack up and serve with maple syrup.

use dairy-free milk

 use lactose-free milk

 use lactose-free milk

 use dairy-free milk and 3 flax eggs instead of the eggs (see TIP on page 168)

- Vegetable oil, for greasing
- 200g (1½ cups) gluten-free self-raising (self-rising) flour
- 1 tsp gluten-free baking powder
- 4 tbsp caster (superfine) sugar
- 200ml (¾ cup plus 1½ tbsp) milk
- 2 tsp vanilla extract
- 3 medium eggs
- 5 handfuls of fresh or frozen blueberries (around 125g/4½oz), plus extra to serve
- Maple syrup, to serve

ONE-SHEET BLUEBERRY PANCAKES

Makes 15 square pancakes ❅
Prep 10 mins **+ Cook** 15 mins

Meet my super-thick and fluffy vanilla pancakes that are packed with bursting blueberries – no flipping required! It's the super-lazy all-in-one breakfast or brunch that's perfect when drenched with maple syrup. Of course, feel free to swap up the blueberries for chocolate chips or slices of ripe banana, if you fancy.

1 Preheat your oven to 180°C fan / 200°C / 400°F. Grease a 28 x 38cm (11 x 15in) baking tray with a little vegetable oil and line with non-stick baking parchment so that there is an overhang around the edges (for lifting it out later).

2 Add the flour, baking powder and sugar to a large mixing bowl and mix until combined. Add the milk and vanilla extract to a jug (pitcher), then crack in the eggs and beat to combine, using a fork.

3 Whisk the egg mixture into the dry ingredients a third at a time, until you have a smooth batter the consistency of thick cream. Pour the batter into the prepared tray and spread out into a flat, even layer. Scatter the blueberries evenly over the top and bake in the oven for 15 minutes.

4 Using the baking parchment, lift the pancake out onto your work surface and use a pizza cutter to cut into 15 squares.

5 Allow to cool for 5 minutes before serving with lots of maple syrup and extra blueberries.

TIP Feel free to swap the blueberries for slices of ripe banana, fresh raspberries, strawberries or a combination of whatever you fancy. You can also replace the berries with chocolate chips too if you'd prefer!

use maple syrup instead of honey

- 4 medium-large very ripe bananas (around 400–460g/ 14–16oz when peeled)
- 120g (4oz) crunchy peanut butter
- 3 tbsp honey or maple syrup
- 85g (3oz) gluten-free puffed rice cereal
- 85g (3oz) gluten-free cornflakes
- 3 tbsp chopped roasted hazelnuts, plus 5–6 tbsp for the top

BANANA NUT CEREAL BARS

Makes 9 ❄

Prep + Cook 30 mins

I think we all know by now that having an emergency gluten-free option on your person at all times is an absolute necessity of life for all gluten-free folks. And when you're off on an early morning mission, I can't emphasize how much less stressful life can be knowing you have one of these in your bag! They're super-soft and chewy, with a lovely crunch from the nuts and an unmissable nutty, banana flavour.

1 Preheat your oven to 160°C fan / 180°C / 350°F. Line a 20cm (8in) square baking tin (pan) with non-stick baking parchment.

2 Mash the bananas in a large mixing bowl, until nice and smooth, then mix in the peanut butter and honey or maple syrup.

3 Stir in the rice cereal and cornflakes until well combined. Mix in the chopped hazelnuts.

4 Spread the mixture into the prepared tin and evenly compact it in. Try to get it nice and level on top before scattering on the extra chopped hazelnuts. Lightly compact those in too, using the back of a fork.

5 Bake in the oven for around 15 minutes. Remove and allow to cool before cutting into bars.

TIP You can also substitute the peanut butter for chocolate hazelnut spread if you're not a huge PB fan.

ensure sausages are low FODMAP

use gluten-free veggie sausages and replace the bacon with ½ a red (bell) pepper, finely diced

---

- Vegetable oil, for greasing
- 4 chipolata sausages
- 4 slices of smoked bacon
- 5 button mushrooms, sliced
- 6 medium eggs
- 1 tsp dried mixed herbs
- 9–10 cherry tomatoes, halved
- Salt and black pepper

To serve (optional)
- Handful of rocket (arugula)
- Ketchup
- Gluten-free brown sauce

ONE-TRAY ALL-DAY BREAKFAST

Serves 4
Prep 5 mins + Cook 25 mins

Imagine throwing the contents of a full English breakfast into a slice-able, herby omelette that'll serve everyone at the table. Then grab a baking tray and go do exactly that! It's a super lazy way to get a hearty breakfast on the table with just 5 minutes of prep required – simply add ketchup or gluten-free brown sauce and get stuck in.

1 Preheat your oven to 220°C fan / 240°C / 465°F.

2 Lightly grease a large baking tray (with sides at least 2.5cm/1in high) with vegetable oil and line with non-stick baking parchment.

3 Arrange the sausages and bacon on the tray, ensuring that the bacon is quite 'creased' and not completely flat on the tray. Place the sliced mushrooms in any remaining gaps. Bake for 10 minutes, or until the bacon is looking nice and crispy around the edges.

4 Meanwhile, crack the eggs into a jug, add the mixed herbs, season with salt and pepper and beat until smooth.

5 Turn the sausages, pour the beaten egg into the tray and arrange the halved cherry tomatoes in any available gaps.

6 Place back in the oven for 15 minutes, or until the sausages are nicely browned and the tomatoes have softened a little.

7 Serve with a little rocket (arugula) on the side and tomato ketchup or gluten-free brown sauce.

use dairy-free milk and cream cheese

 use lactose-free milk and cream cheese

 use lactose-free milk and cream cheese

 use 100g (3½oz) chopped button mushrooms, thinly sliced and lightly pan-fried, instead of smoked salmon

 combine the dairy-free and vegetarian advice, and use a flax egg instead of the egg (see TIP on page 168)

- 130g (1 cup) gluten-free plain (all-purpose) flour
- 2 tsp gluten-free baking powder
- ¼ tsp xanthan gum
- Pinch each of salt and black pepper
- 1 medium egg
- 130ml (½ cup plus 2 tsp) milk
- 2 tbsp butter, melted
- 2 slices of smoked salmon, finely diced
- 3 tbsp cream cheese, plus 6 tsp to top the muffins
- 1 tbsp finely chopped chives

SMOKED SALMON AND CREAM CHEESE BREAKFAST MUFFINS

Makes 6 ✳

Prep 10 mins **+ Cook** 18 mins

Sometimes you never know where the morning will take you, but rest assured that one of these breakfast muffins can always be with you, no matter where you end up. Each muffin is soft and fluffy, with a velvety cream cheese flavour, and rich, smoky salmon in every bite. Enjoy hot or cold, it's up to you.

1 Preheat your oven to 200°C fan / 220°C / 425°F and line a cupcake tray with 6 tulip muffin cases.

2 In a large mixing bowl, combine the flour, baking powder, xanthan gum, salt and pepper. Briefly mix until combined.

3 Crack the egg into a jug (pitcher), then add the milk and melted butter before beating with a fork until smooth.

4 Pour the wet mixture into the dry ingredients and whisk to a smooth batter. Add the smoked salmon, cream cheese and chives. Mix in until evenly dispersed.

5 Spoon around 2 tablespoons of the mixture into each muffin case, ensuring the mixture is evenly split between all six cases. Add a modest teaspoon of cream cheese to the top of each muffin and bake for 15–18 minutes until golden.

6 Transfer to a wire rack to cool to room temperature or just warm. (If you try to remove them from their cases while still hot, you'll lose a lot of your muffin as it'll get stuck to the case!)

LUNCH

As I'm taking the quick and easy concept very seriously, it was very important to me that these recipes wouldn't see you spending as much time or effort as you would to make dinner. Because who wants to feel like they've cooked twice in a day?!

That's why all of these recipes ask for just 10 minutes of effort plus cooking time. What's more, almost all of these recipes are easily portable, meaning if you're not at home for lunch, you can easily take them with you (and heat them up later, if needed).

Of course, this wouldn't be one of my books if I didn't cram it full of all the things that our gluten-free gang truly miss, so expect a few highly requested recipes here too.

use dairy-free milk and cheese

 use lactose-free milk

 use lactose-free milk and omit the tomato relish

 use extra Cheddar instead of pecorino or Parmesan

 use dairy-free milk and cheese, and replace the egg for the batter with 3 tbsp aquafaba (whisked until frothy), and omit the fried eggs

---

- 150g (1 cup plus 2 tbsp) gluten-free self-raising (self-rising) flour
- ½ tsp gluten-free baking powder
- 1 tsp salt
- ½ tsp black pepper, plus extra to serve
- 260ml (1 cup plus 1½ tbsp) milk
- 1 medium egg
- 50g (1¾oz) extra-mature Cheddar, grated
- 20g (¾oz) pecorino or Parmesan, grated
- 3 tbsp finely chopped fresh chives

To serve
- 2 eggs, fried
- 2 tbsp tomato relish
- 2 handfuls of rocket (arugula)

CHEESE AND CHIVE CRISPY WAFFLES

Serves 2 (makes 4 large waffles) ❄
Prep + Cook 15 mins

This recipe was inspired by my last trip to Paris where a gluten-free waffle bar served up the most wonderful savoury waffles, stacked high with all the trimmings. Use my crispy cheese and chive waffle as a base and top with the simple serving suggestion I've provided, or use your own favourite lunch ideas instead.

1 In a large mixing bowl, combine the flour, baking powder, salt and black pepper. In a jug (pitcher), beat together the milk and egg.

2 Create a well in the flour and pour in the milk and egg mixture, whisking thoroughly. After 30 seconds of whisking, the consistency should be nice and smooth. Add the grated cheeses and chives, then mix in until well dispersed.

3 Allow the batter to rest while heating up your waffle maker. All waffle makers vary, so follow the instructions of your particular machine (see TIP below).

4 Once your waffle maker has heated, give the batter one last mix to ensure all the cheese hasn't sunk to the bottom and transfer to the jug you used earlier. Pour half the mixture into your waffle maker, then close the lid.

5 Cook for around 3–4 minutes until golden brown, and lovely and crisp on the outside.

6 Remove from the waffle maker and keep warm in a low oven while you repeat with the remaining batter. Try to avoid stacking them or they'll lose their crispy finish.

7 Place the waffles on serving plates, top with a fried egg and a little coarsely grated black pepper, a dollop of tomato relish and some fresh rocket on the side.

TIP If your waffles keep sticking to the waffle maker, brush it with a little oil before you pour in your batter. My waffle maker is non-stick so I don't really need to, but we also have a cast-iron waffle maker where this step is essential.

use dairy-free cream and a dairy-free cheese/cream cheese

 use lactose-free cream and cream cheese

 use lactose-free cream and cream cheese

 replace the ham with a generous handful of broccoli florets, chopped into small chunks, and steamed or boiled

---

- Vegetable oil, for greasing
- 280g (10oz) store-bought gluten-free puff pastry (see TIP if using homemade)
- 1 egg, beaten

For the quiche

- 3 large eggs
- 200ml (¾ cup plus 1½ tbsp) double (heavy) cream
- ½ tsp each of salt and black pepper
- 50g (1¾oz) thin-cut smoked ham, finely diced
- 50g (1¾oz) extra-mature Cheddar, grated, plus extra for the top
- 1½ tbsp cream cheese
- Small handful of spring onion (scallion) greens, finely chopped

To serve (optional)

- Handful of rocket (arugula)
- Drizzle of extra virgin olive oil

CRUSTLESS CHEESE AND HAM QUICHE WITH PUFF PASTRY HEARTS

Serves 4–6 ❄

Prep 5 mins **+ Cook** 25 mins

I have to admit that, if I saw a crustless quiche on a gluten-free menu, I'd immediately be exclaiming, 'What happened to my pastry?'. And while this is actually super-delicious without the pastry, I couldn't resist finishing it with some incredibly easy-to-make puff pastry hearts to create the full quiche experience. And yes, the filling is actually like a proper quiche, not just an omelette!

1 Preheat your oven to 180°C fan / 200°C / 400°F. Lightly oil a round, 23cm (9in) pie dish and a baking sheet, then line the baking sheet with non-stick baking parchment.

2 Add all the ingredients for the quiche to a large mixing bowl and whisk together until smooth and consistent. Pour into the prepared pie dish and finish with an extra sprinkling of grated cheese. Bake in the oven for 25 minutes.

3 Meanwhile, make the puff pastry hearts. Unroll the pastry onto a work surface. Use a 5cm (2in) heart-shaped cookie cutter to cut out as many hearts as you can, then transfer them to the baking sheet. Brush with beaten egg.

4 After the quiche has been in the oven for 15 minutes, place the puff pastry hearts in the oven and cook for 10 minutes – don't keep the oven door open too long when you place them in!

5 Once done, the quiche should be golden and the pastry hearts slightly puffy and golden. Allow to cool briefly before slicing – the quiche will sink a little during this period, but that's totally normal.

6 Top the quiche with the puff pastry hearts and serve alongside a handful of rocket drizzled with extra virgin olive oil, if you like.

TIP If using homemade gluten-free rough puff pastry (see the recipe in my first or second books), simply roll out to a 20 x 30cm (8 x 12in) rectangle around 3mm (⅛in) thick, and proceed as directed above.

use dairy-free milk and a dairy-free 'buttery' margarine

 use lactose-free milk

 use lactose-free milk, a low FODMAP stock cube and the green parts of the leek only

---

- 4 tbsp butter
- 100g (3½oz) leek, thinly sliced
- 1 medium carrot, cut into 1cm (½in) chunks
- 1 potato, peeled and cut into 1cm (½in) cubes
- 2 tbsp gluten-free plain (all-purpose) flour
- 800ml (3⅓ cups) gluten-free chicken stock
- 200ml (generous ¾ cup) milk
- 3 large or 4 regular boneless, skinless chicken thighs, thinly sliced (about 400g/14oz)
- Handful of fresh parsley, chopped
- Salt and black pepper

Pictured on page 46

WORLD'S BEST* CREAM OF CHICKEN SOUP

Serves 2–3 ❄

Prep + Cook 30 mins

I added the asterisk in the title so I could specify this: *in my totally unbiased opinion. But in all seriousness, this soup has been a favourite in our house for years; I've made it over a hundred times and I wouldn't change a thing. It's creamy, packed full of rich, comforting chicken flavour and it's perfect with gluten-free croutons or crusty gluten-free bread.

1 Place a large, deep saucepan over a medium heat and add the butter. Once melted, add the leek, carrot and potato, then cook, stirring, for 2 minutes. Add the flour, stir in well, and continue to cook for 1 minute.

2 Add the stock and milk, then stir to combine, followed by the sliced chicken. Bring to the boil, then reduce the heat to low and simmer for 20 minutes, or until the carrots and potato are completely softened.

3 Remove the pan from the heat, add the parsley, then blend until smooth and thick, using a stick blender.

4 Season with salt and pepper to taste and serve hot.

use dairy-free cheese

 omit the frankfurter

 omit the frankfurter, use dairy-free cheese and brush the tops with soy milk instead of egg

- 280g (10oz) store-bought gluten-free puff pastry (see TIP if using homemade)
- 1 x 200g (7oz) can baked beans
- 1 gluten-free frankfurter sausage, chopped into 1cm (½in) chunks
- 30g (1oz) extra-mature Cheddar, grated
- 1 egg, beaten

Pictured on page 55

5-INGREDIENT SAUSAGE AND BEAN BAKES

Makes 2 large bakes ❄

Prep 5 mins **+ Cook** 20 mins

There will be no prizes for guessing where the inspiration for this highly requested favourite came from. Here's a clue anyway: it's a bakery where we can't eat 99.9% of everything on sale. These bakes encase melty cheese, beans and sausage in golden, puffy, flaky pastry and couldn't be easier or quicker to make.

1 Preheat your oven to 200°C fan / 220°C / 425°F.

2 Unroll the puff pastry on a work surface and transfer to a large sheet of non-stick baking parchment. Cut in half vertically and horizontally so you're left with 4 rectangles.

3 Open the can of beans and drain off any watery liquid if there is any – too much liquid will see the filling more likely to leak out when baked in the oven.

4 Divide the baked beans between two of the rectangles, leaving a 1cm (½in) gap all around the edge. Divide the chopped frankfurter and grated cheese over the baked beans.

5 Brush beaten egg all around the edges and place the other pastry rectangles on top, gently pressing down on the edges to seal. Crimp the edges using a fork, then arrange both bakes in the middle of the baking parchment, with a 2.5cm (1in) gap between them. Brush all over with the beaten egg. At this point, you're welcome to lightly score wavy lines in the top of the pastry using a small, sharp knife (ensuring you don't actually cut right through the pastry) for the ultimate finishing touch.

6 Using the baking parchment to lift them, transfer to a baking sheet. Bake in the oven for 10-12 minutes until showing signs of turning golden, then cover loosely with foil and bake for a further 8 minutes, until wonderfully golden and puffy.

TIP If using homemade gluten-free rough puff pastry (see the recipe in my first or second books), simply roll out to a 20 x 30cm (8 x 12in) rectangle around 3mm (⅛in) thick, and proceed as directed above.

use dairy-free cheese and cream cheese

 use lactose-free cream cheese

 use lactose-free cream cheese and 100g (3½oz) leek (green parts only) instead of onion

 use dairy-free cheese and cream cheese and brush the tops with soy milk instead of beaten egg

---

- 280g (10oz) store-bought gluten-free puff pastry (see TIP if using homemade)
- 1 egg, beaten

For the filling
- 1 tbsp vegetable oil
- 1 small onion, finely diced
- 225g (8oz) ready-made mashed potato
- 50g (1¾oz) extra-mature Cheddar, grated
- 4 tbsp cream cheese
- 1 tsp salt
- ¼ tsp black pepper

CHEESE AND ONION BAKES

Makes 2 large bakes ❄

Prep 10 mins + **Cook** 20 mins

And yes, I may have also been gazing through the window of a certain bakery only to be reminded of yet another thing I haven't been able to eat in years. I often buy ready-made mashed potato to make this if I'm in a hurry, but feel free to make your own (though it'll almost double the cooking time). Since I can't tolerate onion, I usually make these with leek greens instead.

1 Preheat the oven to 200°C fan/220°C/425°F while you prepare the filling.

2 Place a large frying pan over a medium heat and add the oil. Once hot, add the onion and fry for 4–5 minutes until very slightly browned at the edges.

3 Place the mashed potato in a large mixing bowl, cover and place in the microwave for 2 minutes at full power (900W) until piping hot. Add the grated cheese, cream cheese, salt and pepper, then stir in to combine. Add the cooked onions and stir in until evenly dispersed.

4 Unroll the puff pastry on a work surface and transfer to a large sheet of non-stick baking parchment. Cut in half vertically and horizontally so you're left with 4 rectangles.

5 Divide the mashed potato filling between two of the rectangles, leaving a 1cm (½in) gap around the edges. Brush beaten egg around the edges and place the other pastry rectangles on top, gently pressing down on the edges to seal. Crimp the edges using a fork, then arrange both bakes in the middle of the baking parchment, with a 2.5cm (1in) gap between them. Brush all over with the beaten egg. At this point, you're welcome to lightly score diagonal lines in the top of the pastry using a small, sharp knife (ensuring you don't actually cut right through the pastry) for the ultimate finishing touch.

6 Using the baking parchment to lift them, transfer to a baking sheet. Bake in the oven for 12 minutes until showing signs of turning golden, then cover loosely with foil and bake for a further 8 minutes, until wonderfully golden and puffy.

TIP If using homemade gluten-free rough puff pastry (see the recipe in my first or second books), simply roll out to a 20 x 30cm (8 x 12in) rectangle around 3mm (⅛in) thick, and proceed as directed above.

use a good dairy-free cheese that melts well

 use a low FODMAP BBQ sauce and use oyster mushrooms, thinly sliced, instead of button mushrooms

 make the veggie supreme pizza pocket

 make the veggie supreme pizza pocket using dairy-free cheese

---

- 2 gluten-free pitta breads

For the pizza sauce

- 5 tbsp passata (sieved tomatoes)
- 1 tsp garlic-infused oil
- 1½ tsp gluten-free BBQ sauce, plus extra to serve
- 1 tsp dried oregano
- Pinch each of salt and black pepper

For a BBQ chicken pizza

- 4 slices of cooked chicken breast
- 1 tbsp drained canned sweetcorn
- 1 tbsp spring onion (scallion) greens, chopped
- 30g (1oz) mozzarella, grated

For a tuna feast pizza

- 60g (2oz) drained canned tuna
- 1 tbsp drained canned sweetcorn
- 1 tbsp spring onion (scallion) greens, chopped
- 30g (1oz) extra-mature Cheddar, grated

For a BBQ veggie supreme pizza

- ¼ red (bell) pepper, finely diced
- 5 button mushrooms, thinly sliced
- 1 tbsp spring onion (scallion) greens, chopped
- 30g (1oz) Red Leicester cheese, grated

BBQ PIZZA POCKETS

Serves 2
Prep + Cook 15 mins

Here's my version of something I always see in supermarket frozen aisles, but can never eat: pizza pockets! Each bite is packed full of melty cheese, smoky BBQ flavour and the toppings of your choice, encased in a crisp, folded pitta. This recipe is perfect for using up leftovers and, of course, feel free to use the variations I've provided to inspire your own flavour combos.

1 Preheat your oven to 200°C fan / 220°C / 425°F. Place the pitta breads on a baking sheet.

2 In a small bowl, mix all the ingredients together for the pizza sauce. Spread the sauce onto each pitta, right up to the edges, then add the toppings of your choice, finishing with the cheese.

3 Bake in the oven for 10 minutes, or until the cheese is melted and turning a little golden brown.

4 Drizzle each pizza with extra BBQ sauce, fold in half and serve immediately.

To cook in an air fryer

Preheat the air fryer to 200°C / 400°F. Place the topped pitta in the air fryer basket and spray with a modest amount of garlic-infused oil. Cook for 7–9 minutes or until the cheese is a little golden brown.

use a good dairy-free cheese that melts well

 use lactose-free cheese

 use lactose-free cheese, omit the onion powder and ensure tomato ketchup is low FODMAP

- 1 tbsp vegetable oil, plus extra for greasing
- 500g (1lb 2oz) beef mince (ground beef)
- Generous pinch each of salt and white pepper
- 1 tbsp cornflour (cornstarch) (optional)
- 6 gluten-free tortilla wraps
- 6 slices of processed cheese

For the 'top secret' burger sauce

- 150ml (⅝ cup) mayonnaise
- 2 tsp Dijon mustard
- 2 tbsp gherkins, very finely diced
- 1 tsp caster (superfine) sugar
- ½ tsp smoked paprika
- 1 tsp garlic-infused oil
- 1 tsp onion powder (optional)

To serve

- 6 small handfuls of shredded iceberg lettuce
- 6 slices of pickled gherkins, or more to taste
- 6 tsp tomato ketchup

CHEESEBURGER TOASTADAS

Makes 6
Prep + Cook 20 mins

What if I told you that these taste exactly like a McDonald's Big Mac? Simply take a gluten-free tortilla, top with a square of burger cheese, followed by lightly seasoned beef mince and bake until the tortilla is crispy. Top with my 'top secret' burger sauce, ketchup and all the trimmings and honestly, you wouldn't believe how much this tastes like the real deal.

1 Preheat your oven to 200°C fan / 220°C / 425°F and grease two large baking sheets with a little vegetable oil.

2 In a small dish, mix together all the ingredients for the sauce until well combined.

3 Heat the vegetable oil in a large frying pan over a medium heat. Add the beef mince and salt and white pepper, and fry until nicely browned; if a lot of liquid comes out of the beef, add the cornflour and mix in until it disappears.

4 Place all the tortillas on the baking sheets - if they won't fit then grease a third baking sheet if you have one, or wait until the first batch is done.

5 Top each tortilla with a square of cheese, then top with about 3 heaped tablespoons of beef mince each. Bake in the oven for 5–6 minutes until the beef is a little more golden brown, the cheese has melted and the tortilla looks crispy.

6 Remove from the oven and top each with lettuce, pickled gherkin, a drizzle of the burger sauce and a drizzle of tomato ketchup.

use dairy-free milk and cheese

 use lactose-free milk

 use lactose-free milk

 use dairy-free milk and cheese, and use a flax egg instead of the egg (see TIP on page 168)

- 130g (1 cup) gluten-free plain (all-purpose) flour
- 2 tsp gluten-free baking powder
- ¼ tsp xanthan gum
- ½ tsp salt or celery salt
- ¼ tsp black pepper
- 1 medium egg
- 130ml (½ cup plus 2 tsp) milk
- 2 tbsp olive oil
- ½ red (bell) pepper, diced
- 100g (3½oz) drained canned sweetcorn
- 100g (3½oz) extra-mature Cheddar, grated
- 1 tsp minced chilli paste
- Handful of spring onion (scallion) greens, finely chopped

CHILLI CHEESE MUFFINS

Makes 6 ❄

Prep + Cook 25 mins

These super-moist, cheesy, mildly spicy muffins have totally transformed my opinion of the humble muffin. It's a handy, portable, all-in-one lunch that's delicious hot or cold and 99.9% of the time is far more appealing than any of the gluten-free options I come across when in search of a quick and easy lunch on-the-go.

1 Preheat your oven to 200°C fan / 220°C / 425°F and line a cupcake tray with 6 tulip muffin cases.

2 Add the flour, baking powder, xanthan gum, salt and pepper to a large mixing bowl and briefly mix until combined.

3 Crack the egg into a jug (pitcher), add the milk and olive oil and beat with a fork until smooth.

4 Pour the wet mixture into the dry ingredients and whisk to a smooth batter. Add the red pepper, sweetcorn, grated cheese (reserving a small handful for the tops) chilli paste and spring onion greens. Mix in until evenly dispersed.

5 Spoon around 2 tablespoons of the mixture into each muffin case, dividing it evenly. Sprinkle the reserved grated cheese evenly over the tops and bake for 15–18 minutes until the cheese on top is golden.

6 Transfer to a wire rack to cool to room temperature or just warm. If you try to remove them from their tulip cases while still hot, you'll lose a lot of your muffin as it'll get stuck to the case!

TIP I wouldn't recommend using the pre-grated cheese you can buy in supermarkets for this recipe, as it's usually pre-coated in starch which will dry out the muffin mixture.

use a thick dairy-free yoghurt

 use lactose-free Greek yoghurt

 use lactose-free Greek yoghurt and my garlic and herb dip (page 148) instead of garlic aioli

---

- 200g (scant 1 cup) Greek yoghurt
- 2 tbsp dried mixed herbs
- 1 tbsp red wine vinegar
- 2 tbsp garlic-infused oil
- 2 tbsp lemon juice
- 1 tsp smoked paprika
- 1 tsp ground cumin
- 1 tsp each of salt and black pepper
- 6 boneless, skinless chicken thighs (about 600g/1lb 5oz in total)

To serve
- 3 gluten-free pitta breads, warmed
- Iceberg lettuce, roughly chopped
- Cherry tomatoes, halved
- 2 tbsp garlic aioli, or use the garlic and herb dip (page 148)
- Fresh chives, thinly sliced

CHICKEN GYROS WRAPS

Serves 3 ❋
Prep + Cook 20 mins

Here's a super-simple way of making chicken gyros kebab-style, with no need to marinate for hours and no need to even thread the chicken onto skewers. Simply coat, grill and serve.

1 In a large mixing bowl, combine all the ingredients except the chicken and mix until the spices are evenly distributed. Add the chicken and stir until well coated.

2 Set your oven to a high grill setting. Place the chicken on the rack of a grill pan, ensuring the pan underneath is lined with foil. Grill until the coating is completely dry and a little blackened in places, then flip and repeat. This should take 5–7 minutes each side, depending on how hot your grill gets.

3 Allow to rest for 5 minutes before transferring to a chopping board and slicing into strips.

4 Grab a warm pitta and fill with lettuce, a third of the chicken, some cherry tomatoes and a drizzle of garlic aioli or my garlic and herb dip. Sprinkle with fresh chives, then repeat with the other pittas and serve.

30 MINUTE (OR LESS) FAKEAWAYS

The fakeaways chapter in my first book was dedicated to recreating authentic takeaway food in your own kitchen that nobody would ever know was gluten-free (or not from an actual takeaway).

And this chapter is no different. But this time around, I'm gonna show you how to make it in less time than it would take for a takeaway to arrive at your door – in <u>30 minutes or less</u>.

Not surprisingly, as Mark's family is from Malaysia, he was a huge help in creating this chapter. He never wants to take any credit, but I'm giving him no choice now, so don't forget to thank him too!

There are a lot more fakeaway recipes in my first book *How to Make Anything Gluten Free*, such as prawn toast, sweet and sour chicken/pork/prawn balls and crispy chilli beef that you need to try too. Oh, and make sure you check the speedy sides and party food chapters (pages 130 and 144) for fakeaway sides.

use ½ a 400g (14oz) can of chickpeas (drained) instead of chicken

 follow the vegetarian advice above

- 1 tbsp garlic-infused oil
- 1 medium carrot, thinly sliced lengthways
- 250g (9oz) chicken breast fillets, thinly sliced
- 1 tsp mild curry powder
- ½ tbsp cornflour (cornstarch)
- 1 x 400ml (14fl oz) can coconut milk
- Spring onion (scallion) greens, chopped

For the curry paste
- 2 tbsp crunchy peanut butter
- 2 tbsp gluten-free soy sauce
- 1 tbsp sesame oil (optional)
- ½ tsp minced chilli paste
- 1 tsp caster (superfine) or light brown sugar
- 1 tsp minced lemongrass paste (see TIP)

MARK'S MALAYSIAN CHICKEN SATAY CURRY

Serves 2–3 ❋

Prep + Cook 20 mins

The nutty, creamy and spicy flavours of satay are something Mark discovered as a kid after many family visits to Malaysia. This thick and creamy curry is a tribute to his favourite Malaysian street food and something that we now enjoy almost every week without fail. I'm still in disbelief how quickly he can make this!

1 In a small dish, combine the ingredients for the curry paste (don't worry if it's a little lumpy or separated) and set aside.

2 Add the garlic-infused oil to a large wok and place over a medium-high heat. Once hot, add the carrot and stir-fry until lightly browned. Add the chicken, followed by the curry powder and cornflour, then fry until sealed.

3 Add the curry paste, immediately followed by a third of the coconut milk. Stir well until combined and the peanut butter has melted down to produce a thick sauce. Once bubbling, add the rest of the coconut milk and stir in well.

4 Bring to the boil, then simmer for 5–8 minutes until the sauce is thick and creamy.

5 Top with chopped spring onion greens and serve over sticky jasmine rice.

TIP You can easily find minced lemongrass paste in jars or tubes in the spice aisle of supermarkets.

use a 300g (10½oz) block of extra-firm tofu (sliced into wide, thin strips) instead of chicken

follow the vegetarian advice above

- Vegetable oil, for frying
- 400g (14oz) chicken mini fillets
- 70g (generous ½ cup) cornflour (cornstarch)
- 1 tsp salt
- Handful of spring onion (scallion) greens, chopped, to serve

For the sauce
- Juice of 2 small lemons (6 tbsp)
- 215ml (1 cup minus 2 tbsp) water
- 6 tbsp caster (superfine) sugar
- ½ tsp minced ginger paste
- ¼ tsp dried chilli flakes
- 2½ tbsp cornflour (cornstarch), mixed with 5 tbsp water

Pictured overleaf

CRISPY LEMON CHICKEN

Serves 3 ❄

Prep + Cook 25 mins

This takeaway classic pairs crispy chicken with a thick, sweet and zesty lemon sauce, and couldn't be easier or quicker to make from scratch. It simply involves coating chicken in cornflour (cornstarch) and frying, then bringing your sauce to a boil and adding a cornflour slurry. A bit of minor multitasking goes a long way here, but if I can do it, then you definitely can!

1 Pour vegetable oil into a large frying pan to around a 1cm (½in) depth. A large pan is key to making this super-fast, otherwise you'll have to fry your chicken in two separate batches, which of course takes twice as long. Place over a medium-high heat until the oil reaches 170°C (340°F); test the temperature with a cooking thermometer, or using the wooden spoon handle test (see page 16).

2 While the oil is heating, add the chicken, cornflour and salt to a large mixing bowl and toss until well coated, squeezing the chicken and compacting the flour to it as much as you can – the more, the better! Place to one side.

3 Grab a large wok and add all the sauce ingredients except the cornflour. Place over a medium heat, bring to the boil, then simmer for 3–4 minutes.

4 Once the oil is hot enough, carefully add your coated chicken – it should sizzle nicely. Cook for 2½ minutes on each side, or until the crispy coating starts to turn a little golden. Remove with a slotted spoon and place on a wire rack set over a baking tray to drain.

5 After your sauce has simmered, drizzle your cornflour and water mixture into the wok and stir in immediately, then simmer until the sauce thickens.

6 Finally, add your crispy chicken to the wok, briefly stir and serve immediately topped with spring onion greens. Serve with a microwavable packet of rice, for ease, or pineapple and cashew nut fried rice (page 135) for the ultimate fakeaway experience.

Got an extra 5 minutes? Once the chicken has been fried and placed on the wire rack to drain, place back in the hot oil for another 3–4 minutes. This makes it even more crispy!

use a low FODMAP curry powder in the seasoning mix

 use 1 medium carrot (sliced into thin strips) and 2 handfuls of button mushrooms (thinly sliced) instead of using chicken and prawns

 follow the vegetarian advice and crumble in 125g (4½oz) of extra-firm tofu (instead of the eggs) with a pinch of turmeric

---

- 2 tbsp garlic-infused oil, plus extra for drizzling
- 1 red (bell) pepper, cut into thin strips
- 1 chicken breast fillet, thinly sliced
- 2 large eggs
- 85g (3oz) pre-cooked king prawns (shrimp)
- 1 tsp thinly sliced fresh red chilli or ¼ tsp dried chilli flakes, plus extra to serve (optional)
- 300g (10½oz) fresh vermicelli rice noodles
- Handful of beansprouts
- Handful of spring onion (scallion) greens

For the seasoning mix
- 1 tsp gluten-free soy sauce
- 1 tsp mild curry powder
- ½ tsp ground turmeric
- ½ tsp minced ginger paste
- 1 tsp caster (superfine) sugar
- 2 tbsp water
- ¼ tsp salt

Pictured overleaf

SINGAPORE NOODLES

Serves 3
Prep + Cook 15 mins

Hands down, this was my favourite dish to order from our local Chinese takeaway back when I could still eat gluten. I was absolutely addicted to those mildly spicy, curry-tinged noodles, packed with prawns and chicken. So how sad is it that I went almost an entire decade without ever eating it? Fortunately, it's incredibly simple and speedy to whip up at home and, thanks to the spice blend, you'd never know it was homemade.

1 Combine the ingredients for the seasoning mix in a small bowl and set aside.

2 Place a large wok over a high heat and add the garlic-infused oil. Once hot, add the red pepper and stir-fry for a minute or so. Add the chicken and fry until sealed.

3 Create a well in the middle of the wok and crack in both eggs. Break the yolks and allow to sit for a minute or so before turning over. Break the egg up into small chunks, then add the cooked prawns to the wok and stir-fry for 1–2 minutes. Add the fresh chilli or chilli flakes, if using.

4 Add the fresh rice noodles and drizzle a little more garlic-infused oil over them, then add the beansprouts and toss everything together until evenly dispersed.

5 Lastly, add the seasoning mix and keep stir-frying for 2 minutes until everything is evenly coated. Finish with chopped spring onion greens and more thinly sliced red chilli or dried chilli flakes, if using.

Got an extra 5 minutes? Buy dried rather than fresh vermicelli noodles, and soak them in boiling water for 5 minutes, then drain, before adding to the wok. It's quicker to use fresh, but I find they often break up a lot more than dried.

use carrot instead of onion and use only the heads (not the stalks) of the broccoli; use miso paste instead of oyster sauce

- 150g (5oz) broccoli florets (about 1 small head of broccoli), cut into bite-sized pieces
- 2 tbsp garlic-infused oil
- ½ tsp dried chilli flakes
- ¼ onion, diced, or 1 small carrot, thinly sliced
- 1 tsp white miso paste (ensure gluten-free) or 2 tbsp gluten-free oyster sauce
- 3 tbsp gluten-free soy sauce
- 2 tbsp dark brown sugar
- 1 tbsp dry sherry
- 300g (10½oz) fresh vermicelli rice noodles
- Handful of beansprouts
- 2 tbsp toasted sesame seeds, to finish

For the beef

- 250g (9oz) beef sirloin (rump) steak, thinly sliced
- 2 tbsp gluten-free soy sauce
- 1 tbsp dry sherry
- 1 tbsp cornflour (cornstarch)
- ½ tsp bicarbonate of soda (baking soda)

Pictured on page 68

SIZZLING BEEF AND BROCCOLI STIR FRY

Serves 2

Prep + Cook 20 mins

Who ordered tender strips of beef and noodles coated in a sticky and savoury sauce with chunks of broccoli? Everyone? Well, it'll be ready in about 20 minutes!

1 Add the beef, soy sauce, sherry, cornflour and bicarbonate of soda to a small bowl, mix until well coated and set aside.

2 Pop the broccoli florets into a small microwave-safe bowl, fill just under halfway with boiling water and cover with a side plate. Pop into the microwave at full power (900W) for 3 minutes, or until perfectly cooked. Drain and set aside.

3 Add the garlic-infused oil to a large wok and place over a medium-high heat. Once hot, add the chilli flakes and onion or carrot and stir-fry for 3–4 minutes, or until lightly browned. Add the coated beef and stir-fry until sealed, then add the miso paste or oyster sauce and stir-fry until evenly dispersed.

4 Add the soy sauce, sugar and sherry and stir until everything is well coated and the sauce is bubbling. Lastly, add the cooked broccoli florets, rice noodles and beansprouts.

5 Toss everything in the wok for a couple of minutes until evenly dispersed and heated through, before finishing with a sprinkle of sesame seeds.

6 Optionally serve with crispy seaweed (page 134), salt and pepper chips (page 138) or veggie spring rolls (page 157).

use green (bell) pepper instead
of red and use a low FODMAP
sweet chilli sauce

 use a 250g (9oz) block of extra-
firm tofu, cut into 2cm (¾in)
long strips, instead of the chicken

- Vegetable oil, for frying
- 1 small egg
- ¼ tsp salt
- 250g (9oz) chicken breast mini
  fillets, chopped into thin strips
  1cm (½in) wide
- 60g (½ cup) cornflour
  (cornstarch)
- 1 red or green (bell) pepper (or
  half of both), cut into thin strips
- 250ml (1 cup) mild sweet chilli
  sauce (ensure gluten-free)
- 1 tbsp gluten-free soy sauce
- 1 tsp minced ginger paste
- Handful of spring onion (scallion)
  greens, chopped, to serve

Pictured on page 69

SHREDDED CRISPY CHILLI CHICKEN

Serves 2 ❄
Prep + Cook 25 mins

This recipe is the epitome of a lightning-fast fakeaway: simply coat and fry the chicken, then fry the pepper and smother the lot in sweet chilli sauce. The sticky, sweet and spicy sauce envelops that crunchy, crispy chicken and even though you didn't need to make it, you can still take all the credit for it. Consider this your permission to do so.

1 Pour vegetable oil into a large frying pan to around a 1cm (½in) depth. Place over a medium heat until it reaches 180°C (350°F). If you don't have a digital food thermometer, check the temperature of the oil using the wooden spoon handle test (page 16). Line a large plate with kitchen paper, ready for later.

2 Meanwhile, crack the egg into a large mixing bowl and briefly beat with a fork, before adding the salt and chicken strips. Toss until well coated, then mix in the cornflour.

3 Grab a large wok, add 1 tablespoon vegetable oil and place over a medium-high heat. Once hot, add the pepper strips and stir-fry for 2–3 minutes. Next, add the sweet chilli sauce, soy sauce and minced ginger and mix well. Bring to the boil, then keep over a very low heat while you cook the chicken.

4 Once the oil in the frying pan is hot enough, carefully lower the chicken strips into the oil, two at a time, using a pair of small tongs – they should sizzle nicely. Cook for 4–5 minutes, turning halfway, or until the crispy coating starts to turn a little golden. Remove with a slotted spoon and place on the plate lined with kitchen paper to drain. If you have a little more time, heat the oil a little more, then return the chicken to the oil for 2–3 minutes, then drain once more.

5 Add the crispy chicken to the wok, briefly stir and serve topped with spring onion greens. Serve with a microwavable packet of rice for ease, or pineapple and cashew nut fried rice (page 135).

replace the chicken or prawns with thinly sliced mushrooms and fry in the hot oil

- 3 tbsp garlic-infused oil
- 100g (3½oz) chicken breast fillet, thinly sliced, or cooked king prawns (shrimp)
- 3 tbsp frozen peas
- Sweet chilli sauce, to serve

For the egg mixture
- 5 large eggs
- 1 tbsp gluten-free soy sauce
- 1 tbsp sesame oil
- 1 tsp sugar
- ¼ tsp salt
- 2 tsp water
- Handful of spring onion (scallion) greens, sliced

KING PRAWN OR CHICKEN FOO YUNG

Serves 2

Prep + Cook 10 mins

This is our go-to recipe when we need a super-speedy dinner and, dare I say it: it tastes better than the one I remember ordering from my local Chinese takeaway. Think chunky egg, packed with peas, spring onion (scallion) and your choice of prawns (shrimp) or chicken, topped with a sweet and spicy sweet chilli sauce. It simply tastes too good to have been made in 10 minutes.

1 Crack the eggs into a medium mixing bowl, then add the soy sauce, sesame oil, sugar, salt, water and chopped spring onion greens. Mix until smooth and combined.

2 Place a large wok over a high heat and add the garlic-infused oil. If using chicken, once the oil is hot, add the chicken and stir-fry until sealed, followed by the frozen peas. Briefly fry until the peas are bright and green. If using cooked prawns, add the peas and prawns at the same time and stir-fry for 30 seconds.

3 Pour in the egg mixture and immediately stir so that the peas and prawns/chicken are evenly dispersed.

4 Gently stir occasionally to create a chunkier texture (or it will form a very flat, more omelette-like texture). After 2 minutes, use a spatula to break the omelette up into quarters, then flip and fry for a further minute.

5 To serve, drizzle a little sweet chilli sauce or gluten-free dark soy sauce (a recipe for homemade is in my first book *How to Make Anything Gluten Free*) on top.

TIP Make this recipe your own - it's a great recipe for using up any leftovers lurking in your fridge! Also, you can add whatever veg you like, just ensure you fry them at the beginning until slightly softened; red (bell) pepper and mushrooms work especially well here.

swap the cashew nuts for roasted peanuts (ensure gluten-free)

use 250g (9oz) extra-firm tofu (chopped into bite-sized pieces) instead of chicken or pork and ensure the sherry is veggie/vegan-friendly

follow the vegetarian advice above

- Vegetable oil, for frying
- 250g (9oz) pork tenderloin, thinly sliced, or 250g (9oz) chicken breast, chopped into bite-sized pieces
- 1 tbsp gluten-free soy sauce
- ½ tsp white pepper
- 1 tbsp cornflour (cornstarch)
- ½ tsp bicarbonate of soda (baking soda)
- 1 tbsp garlic-infused oil
- 1 red (bell) pepper, chopped into bite-sized pieces
- 1 tbsp minced ginger paste
- 1 tbsp Szechuan peppercorns, crushed, or black peppercorns, coarsely ground
- 1 tbsp dry sherry
- Big handful of cashew nuts
- 1 tsp dried chilli flakes, to serve (optional)

Pictured on page 69

SZECHUAN CRISPY PORK OR CHICKEN

Serves 3 ❄

Prep + Cook 25 mins

If you loved the crispy salt and pepper chicken recipe in my first book, then you absolutely must try this classic too. Crispy chicken or pork strips, cashew nuts and red pepper get a tongue-tingling mild-medium heat, with the Szechuan peppercorns and dry sherry adding an aromatic flavour that's truly unique. You can find Szechuan peppercorns in the spice aisle, but make sure you grind them first if whole, or pop them into a pepper grinder instead.

1 Pour vegetable oil into a large frying pan to around a 1cm (½in) depth. Place over a medium heat until it reaches 180°C (350°F). If you don't have a digital food thermometer, check the temperature of the oil using the wooden spoon handle test (page 16).

2 Add the pork or chicken to a small bowl with the soy sauce, white pepper, cornflour and bicarbonate of soda. Mix until well coated and set aside.

3 Once the oil has reached the desired temperature, carefully lower all of the coated pork or chicken pieces into the oil, a couple at a time, using a pair of small tongs – it should sizzle nicely. Cook for 4–5 minutes, turning halfway, or until the coating starts to turn golden.

4 Remove with a slotted spoon and place on a wire rack set over a baking tray to drain. If you have a little more time, return the pork or chicken to the hot oil for 2–3 minutes, then drain once more.

5 Place a large wok over a medium-high heat and add the garlic-infused oil. Once hot, add the red pepper and stir-fry until lightly browned, then add the minced ginger. Add the cooked pork or chicken, immediately followed by the Szechuan pepper or ground black pepper, and stir in. Stir-fry until everything is well coated, then add the sherry, which should almost instantly disappear if your wok is hot enough.

6 Throw in the cashew nuts, stir and sprinkle with chilli flakes, if you like a little extra heat. Serve with a microwavable packet of rice for ease, or pineapple and cashew nut fried rice (page 135) for the ultimate fakeaway experience.

use 1 medium carrot (thinly sliced) instead of a red (bell) pepper, and use low FODMAP tomato ketchup

use extra-firm tofu instead of chicken

follow the vegetarian advice above

- 250g (9oz) chicken breast or extra-firm tofu, chopped into 2.5cm (1in) chunks
- 2 tbsp cornflour (cornstarch)
- ½ tsp salt
- 4 tbsp garlic-infused oil
- 1 red (bell) pepper, chopped
- 1 tbsp minced ginger paste
- ½ tbsp cornflour (cornstarch), mixed with 2 tbsp water
- 1 tbsp sesame seeds, to finish

For the sauce
- 3 tbsp gluten-free soy sauce
- 2 tbsp light or dark brown sugar
- 1 tbsp tomato ketchup
- 1 tbsp rice wine vinegar
- 1 tbsp toasted sesame oil
- 1 tsp minced chilli paste
- ½ tsp five spice

GENERAL TSO'S CHICKEN OR TOFU

Serves 2 ❄

Prep + Cook 15 mins

This takeaway classic is super-easy to throw together using ingredients that most people probably have lurking in the cupboards already. With your choice of chicken or tofu (no shallow-frying required) this sweet and savoury favourite can be on your plate in just 15 minutes.

1 In a small bowl, mix all the ingredients for the sauce together until smooth.

2 Put the chopped chicken or tofu, cornflour and salt into a medium mixing bowl and toss until well coated.

3 Place a wok over a medium-high heat and add the garlic-infused oil. Once hot, add the chicken or tofu and stir-fry for 1–2 minutes before adding the red pepper and ginger paste. Continue to stir-fry until the chicken is cooked or the tofu is golden and the pepper is slightly browned.

4 Next, add the sauce and let it sit until it's nicely bubbling, then lower the heat and simmer for 30 seconds. Add the cornflour mixture and immediately stir in. The sauce should be a thick and sticky consistency after 1–2 minutes simmering. Top with sesame seeds and serve with a microwavable packet of rice for ease, or pineapple and cashew nut fried rice (page 135) for the ultimate fakeaway experience.

use light brown sugar instead of honey

- 2 skin-on salmon fillets (240g/8½oz in total)

For the sauce

- 2 tbsp gluten-free soy sauce
- 2 tbsp mirin or rice wine vinegar
- 2 tbsp dry sherry or sake
- 1½ tbsp light brown sugar or honey
- 1 tbsp garlic-infused oil, plus extra for drizzling
- 1 tsp minced ginger paste
- 1 tsp cornflour (cornstarch)

To serve

- 2 x 250g (9oz) packets of microwavable rice or 500g (1lb 2oz) cooked rice
- Handful of spring onion (scallion) greens, finely chopped
- Juice of ½ lime
- 1 pak choi, steamed for 3 minutes

STICKY TERIYAKI SALMON

Serves 2

Prep + Cook 25 mins

Everyone needs a recipe like this amidst a busy, hectic week. Store-cupboard ingredients shine here yet again, instantly transforming two plain fillets of oven-baked salmon into a fiesta of teriyaki flavour. Just cook the salmon, then roll around in the sauce – simple.

To cook the salmon in the oven

Preheat your oven to 200°C fan / 220°C / 425°F. Drizzle a little garlic-infused oil over a small baking tray, then add the salmon. Turn the salmon to ensure an even coating of oil on all sides, then pop into the oven skin-side up for 15 minutes until the skin is slightly golden and crispy.

To cook the salmon in an air fryer

Preheat the air fryer to 200°C (400°F) and spray a little garlic-infused oil into the tray. Place the salmon in the air fryer basket and spray with a modest amount of garlic-infused oil. Cook for 8–10 minutes, or until the skin is crispy and golden.

1 Combine all the ingredients for the sauce in a small bowl or jug (pitcher). Mix well until smooth and no cornflour is visible. Set aside. Prepare your rice according to the packet instructions, then keep warm.

2 When your salmon is a few minutes away from being done, place a small frying pan over a medium heat. Once hot, add the sauce and bring to the boil until nicely bubbling, then turn down to a low heat.

3 Immediately add the cooked salmon to the pan and allow to sit for a minute or so before flipping over and cooking for another minute. Turn the salmon onto its side and spoon more of the sauce on top, before flipping and repeating. It's done when there is a thick and sticky coating all over the salmon fillets.

4 To serve, mix the spring onion greens into the rice and squeeze the lime juice over it. Mix briefly and serve with the salmon on top with steamed pak choi on the side.

use a veggie/vegan meat-free mince instead of pork

 follow the vegetarian advice above

- 300g (10½oz) fresh vermicelli rice noodles or 100g (3½oz) dried vermicelli rice noodles
- 2 tbsp garlic-infused oil
- 400g (14oz) pork mince (ground pork), around 12% fat
- 100g (3½oz) carrot, thinly sliced
- 1 tbsp cornflour (cornstarch)
- ½ tsp ground ginger
- ¼ tsp five spice
- ¼ tsp salt
- ½ tsp white pepper
- 1 tbsp dark brown sugar
- 1½ tbsp gluten-free soy sauce
- 1 small little gem lettuce, shredded
- 1 tbsp sesame oil, plus extra for drizzling
- Handful of sliced spring onion (scallion) greens

YUK SUNG STIR FRY

Serves 2

Prep + Cook 15 mins

Meet the Chinese takeaway starter that just graduated into a full-on stir fry. Traditionally served as minced/ground pork (seasoned to taste a lot like Peking duck) wrapped in lettuce leaves and topped with rice noodles, this recipe incorporates all of those elements into an all-in-one meal that takes just 15 minutes to make.

1 Prepare the rice noodles according to the packet instructions. Keep warm until later.

2 Add the garlic-infused oil to a large wok and place over a medium-high heat. Add the pork mince and fry for 3–4 minutes until no longer pink. Add the carrot and continue to fry for 2 minutes before adding the cornflour.

3 Mix everything until the cornflour disappears, then add the ginger, five spice, salt, white pepper, sugar and soy sauce. Stir to combine, then stir-fry for a further 2–3 minutes until any liquid has evaporated. Stir in the lettuce and sesame oil.

4 Place the prepared rice noodles on two serving plates and drizzle around 1 teaspoon of sesame oil over each. Toss the noodles briefly until well coated. Place a generous amount of the pork on top and finish with a sprinkling of sliced spring onion greens.

use a veggie/vegan alternative to fish sauce and use baby corn/ mangetout instead of chicken

follow the vegetarian advice above

- 2 tbsp garlic-infused oil
- 1 small aubergine (eggplant), sliced 1cm (½in) thick
- 1 x 400ml (14fl oz) can coconut milk
- 250g (9oz) boneless, skinless chicken thighs, sliced, or 150g (5oz) baby corn (chopped into bite-sized pieces) and 100g (3½oz) mangetout
- 1 tbsp cornflour (cornstarch) mixed with 2 tbsp water
- Handful of spring onion (scallion) greens, chopped
- Fresh green chilli, sliced (optional)

For the curry paste

- 1 tbsp minced ginger or galangal paste
- ½ tsp dried chilli flakes
- 1 tsp minced lemongrass paste
- 1 tbsp ground cumin
- 1½ tsp minced coriander (cilantro) paste
- 1 tbsp garlic-infused oil or ½ tsp minced garlic paste
- 1 tbsp fish sauce
- 1 tbsp lime juice
- 1 tbsp brown sugar

MARK'S JADE CHICKEN OR VEGGIE CURRY

Serves 2–3 ❄

Prep + Cook 30 mins

Here's Mark's version of a Thai green curry that's thick and creamy, with an easy veggie option too. It's packed with tender chicken and the aubergine (eggplant) soaks up all that sauce, which has an amazing depth of sweet and sour flavours. Plus, there's no need to blend the paste before using!

1 In a small bowl, combine all the ingredients for the curry paste and set aside.

2 Add the garlic-infused oil to a large wok and place over a medium heat. Once hot, add the aubergine and fry until slightly browned on both sides. Pour in a third of the coconut milk (stir it in the can first as it can often dramatically separate) and bring to the boil. Add your curry paste, stir in and fry until the mixture has slightly thickened.

3 Add your choice of chicken thighs or baby corn/mangetout and allow to cook for 1–2 minutes before adding the rest of the coconut milk. Bring down to a simmer and cook for 10–15 minutes.

4 Lastly, add the cornflour mixture and immediately stir in until the sauce thickens a little.

5 Top with chopped spring onion greens and sliced chilli, if using, and serve with sticky jasmine rice or rice noodles.

TIP Double or treble the quantities of the curry paste and store in the fridge in an airtight container for up to 2 weeks. Simply use 2½ tablespoons of the paste whenever you fancy making this for a very quick and easy meal! You can easily find minced galangal paste, minced lemongrass paste and minced coriander paste in jars or tubes in the spice or herb aisle of supermarkets.

use vegetable oil instead of butter

 use a 400g (14oz) can of chickpeas (drained) instead of chicken

 combine the dairy free and vegetarian advice

- 2 tbsp butter
- 400g (14oz) chicken breast fillet, chopped into 2.5cm (1in) chunks
- 200ml (generous ¾ cup) passata (sieved tomatoes)
- 250ml (1 cup) boiling water
- 60g (2oz) creamed coconut block
- 1 tsp salt
- Big handful of spinach, roughly chopped

For the curry paste
- 2 tbsp garlic-infused oil
- 2 tsp minced ginger paste
- ½ tsp black pepper
- 1½ tsp garam masala
- ½ tsp ground turmeric
- 2 tbsp desiccated (dried shredded) coconut
- 3 tbsp ground almonds
- 1 tsp ground cumin
- 1 tsp ground coriander

QUICK CHICKEN KORMA

Serves 2 ❄

Prep + Cook 15 mins

This is the definition of a curry in a hurry, and your spice cupboard is definitely your friend for this one. Once you've got the spice blend together, you're already halfway to a creamy korma with oceans of depth and mild spice. We like to add chopped spinach to ours to make it a more well-rounded meal, but feel free to add whatever pre-cooked veg you like.

1 In a small dish, combine all the ingredients for the curry paste.

2 Place a large pan over a medium heat and add the butter. Once melted, add the chicken and fry for 1 minute before adding the curry paste. Fry until the chicken is sealed and the spices are fragrant.

3 Add the passata, boiling water, creamed coconut block and salt. Stir to combine and bring to the boil, then simmer for 7-8 minutes, or until the chicken is cooked and the sauce has thickened. Add the spinach, stir in and allow to bubble for a minute or so.

4 Serve with basmati rice, speedy naan bread (page 142) and some of my veggie pakoras (page 156).

use 250g (9oz) extra-firm tofu (chopped into bite-sized pieces) instead of chicken

- Vegetable oil, for frying
- 1 small egg
- 250g (9oz) chicken breast fillet, chopped into 2.5cm (1in) strips
- ¼ tsp salt
- 60g (½ cup) cornflour (cornstarch)
- 2 tsp sesame seeds
- Handful of spring onion (scallion) greens, chopped

For the sauce
- 2 tsp minced ginger paste
- ¼ tsp dried chilli flakes
- 60g (5 tbsp) brown sugar
- 100ml (scant ½ cup) smooth orange juice
- 4 tbsp gluten-free soy sauce
- 4 tbsp rice wine vinegar
- 1 tbsp cornflour (cornstarch) mixed with 2 tbsp water

MARK'S CRISPY ORANGE CHICKEN

Serves 2 ❄
Prep + Cook 25 mins

About two decades ago when on holiday in Florida (back when I could eat gluten), I had the most amazing orange chicken at Panda Express. It was crispy, sweet and sticky, much like sweet and sour but with an orange flavour that made it something else entirely. Fortunately, almost 20 years since I last ate it, Mark recreated it for me and it tastes even better than I remember!

1 Pour vegetable oil into a large frying pan to around a 1cm (½in) depth. Place over a medium heat until it reaches 180°C (350°F). If you don't have a digital food thermometer, check the temperature of the oil using the wooden spoon handle test (page 16). Line a large plate with kitchen paper, ready for later.

2 In a bowl, mix together all the ingredients for the sauce except the cornflour mixture, and set aside.

3 Crack the egg into a large mixing bowl and briefly beat with a fork, then add the chicken and salt. Toss until the chicken is coated in egg, then add the cornflour and briefly mix in until well coated.

4 Once the oil is hot enough, lower the chicken strips into the oil, two at a time, using a pair of small tongs – they should sizzle nicely. Cook for 4–5 minutes, turning halfway, or until the crispy coating starts to turn a little golden. Remove with a slotted spoon and place on the plate lined with kitchen paper. If you have a little more time, return the chicken to the hot oil for 2–3 minutes, then drain once more.

5 Grab a large wok and place over a medium-high heat. Once hot, add the sauce and bring to a bubble. Allow to bubble for 30 seconds, then reduce the heat and simmer for 30 more seconds, before stirring in the cornflour mixture. It should now be nice and thick.

6 Add the crispy chicken to the wok, briefly stir and serve immediately topped with the sesame seeds and spring onion greens. Either serve with a microwavable packet of rice, or pineapple and cashew nut fried rice (page 135) for the ultimate fakeaway experience.

ensure sausages are FODMAP-friendly

 use gluten-free veggie sausages

 use gluten-free vegan sausages

- Vegetable oil, for frying
- 125g (1 cup minus 1 tbsp) gluten-free plain (all-purpose) flour
- ½ tsp gluten-free baking powder
- 1 tsp salt
- 150ml (⅝ cup) gluten-free beer or carbonated water
- 6 gluten-free pork sausages

CHIP-SHOP-STYLE BATTERED SAUSAGES

Serves 3 ❄

Prep + Cook 25 mins

Who knew this chip-shop classic could be recreated so quickly and easily at home? Simply whip up a slightly thicker version of my crispy gluten-free beer batter, dredge the sausages and pop into hot oil. All that's left to do is serve with chips and lots of ketchup.

1 Add vegetable oil to a deep, large saucepan or a heavy-based wok until around a third full. Place over a medium heat until it reaches 170°C (340°F). If you don't have a digital food thermometer, check the temperature of the oil using the wooden spoon handle test (page 16). Line a large plate with kitchen paper, ready for later.

2 In a large mixing bowl, combine the flour, baking powder and salt, and mix until well combined. Add the beer or water and mix until thick and smooth.

3 Once the oil has reached the desired temperature, use a pair of tongs to turn three of the sausages in the mixture until they have a lovely, thick coating, then quickly (and carefully) transfer to the hot oil. Cook for 7–10 minutes until the batter is golden and the sausages are a little browned in places, turning occasionally. Once cooked, transfer to the plate lined with kitchen paper to drain.

4 Repeat using your remaining three sausages.

5 Serve with oven chips, for ease, or use my air fryer chips recipe on page 139.

TIP If your sausages are getting stuck to the bottom of the pan or wok, then it's likely that your oil isn't hot enough. If your coating isn't nice and crispy after 7–10 minutes this could be the cause too.

omit the onion and garlic powder

 use king oyster mushrooms (sliced into strips) instead of chicken

 follow the vegetarian advice, then use 100ml (scant ½ cup) dairy-free milk mixed with 1 tsp lemon juice instead of the eggs; allow to rest for 10 minutes and continue with the recipe as directed

---

- 500g (1lb 2oz) chicken mini fillets
- Vegetable oil, for frying
- 2 large eggs

For the coating

- 230g (1¾ cups) gluten-free plain (all-purpose) flour
- 2 tsp dried thyme
- 2 tsp dried basil
- 1½ tsp dried oregano
- 1 tbsp celery salt
- 1 tbsp dried mustard powder
- 2 tbsp smoked paprika
- 1 tbsp ground ginger
- 1 tbsp white pepper
- 1 tsp onion powder (optional)
- 1 tsp garlic powder (optional)

GLUTEN-FREE BONELESS BANQUET

Serves 2-3 ❄

Prep + Cook 30 mins

Colonel Excell is back with another gluten-free fried chicken feast! This time it's a selection of boneless chicken tenders and popcorn chicken in a crispy coating that genuinely tastes like it's from a certain fast-food chain that's never gluten-free. Shallow-fry for the best results, or use an air fryer for a healthier, yet still very crispy alternative.

1 Chop around a third of the chicken fillets into 2cm (¾in) cubes.

2 Pour vegetable oil into a large frying pan to around a 1cm (½in) depth. Place over a medium heat until it reaches 180°C (350°F). If you don't have a digital food thermometer, check the temperature of the oil using the wooden spoon handle test (page 16). Line a large plate with kitchen paper, ready for later.

3 While the oil is heating, mix together the coating ingredients in a large bowl. Crack the eggs into another large bowl and briefly beat with a fork. Add the chicken strips and diced chicken to the egg and mix thoroughly until well coated. Transfer to the dry coating ingredients bowl and toss until well coated with no bare spots.

4 Once the oil is hot enough, take the large, coated strips of chicken and carefully lower them into the oil using a pair of small tongs – they should sizzle nicely. Cook for 7-8 minutes, turning halfway, or until the crispy coating starts to turn golden. Remove with a slotted spoon and place on the plate lined with kitchen paper.

5 Repeat with your diced chicken, cooking for 5 minutes and turning halfway, then transfer to the plate lined with kitchen paper.

6 Serve with chips, mini corn-on-the-cob and gluten-free BBQ sauce or ketchup.

To cook in an air fryer:

Preheat your air fryer to 200°C (400°F) and generously spray the basket with vegetable oil. Once coated in the egg and the flour mixture, place as many of the chicken strips into the air fryer as will comfortably fit without overlapping. Spray generously with oil once more - not enough oil and the finished result will look white and powdery. Cook for 7-8 minutes, turning halfway through, until the coating is golden and crisp, then repeat with the remaining chicken, cooking for 5 minutes.

use dairy-free 'buttery' margarine

 use maple syrup instead of honey, then omit the garlic paste and instead mix in 1 tbsp garlic-infused oil before serving

 use 400g (14oz) extra-firm tofu (cut into 1cm/½in strips) instead of chicken

 follow the vegetarian advice, but use maple syrup instead of honey

---

- 100g (⅘ cup) cornflour (cornstarch) or potato starch
- 1 tsp bicarbonate of soda (baking soda)
- ½ tsp salt
- 400g (14oz) chicken breast mini fillets
- Vegetable oil, for frying
- Handful of spring onion greens, chopped

For the sauce

- 2 tbsp butter
- 1 tbsp minced ginger paste
- 2 tsp minced garlic paste
- 2 tbsp gluten-free soy sauce
- 3 tbsp rice wine vinegar
- 70ml (scant ⅓ cup) honey
- ½ tsp dried chilli flakes, plus extra to finish

HONEY GARLIC CHICKEN TENDERS

Serves 2 ❄

Prep + Cook 25 mins

I can't imagine a finer combination than crispy chicken in a sweet, spicy, sticky honey and garlic sauce. The ingredients needed are so humble, yet forge such big, bold flavours that I know everyone will love. Plus, using mini fillets means there's no need to even chop the chicken!

1 In a large mixing bowl, mix the cornflour (or potato starch) with the bicarbonate of soda and salt. Add the chicken mini fillets and toss around until well coated in the starch. Try your best to squeeze the chicken and compact the flour to it as much as you can.

2 Pour vegetable oil into a large frying pan to around a 1cm (½in) depth. Place over a medium heat for 5 minutes or until it reaches 180°C (350°F). If you don't have a digital food thermometer, use the wooden spoon handle test (page 16).

3 Carefully lower half of the coated chicken strips into the oil – they should sizzle nicely. Cook for around 10 minutes, flipping them halfway, or until the crispy coating starts to turn golden. Once cooked, remove from the oil and place on a wire rack set over a baking tray to drain. Repeat with the other half of the coated chicken.

4 For the sauce, place a large wok over a medium heat and add the butter. Once melted, add the ginger and garlic pastes and stir-fry until the butter starts to brown a little. Next, add the soy sauce and vinegar, bring to the boil, then add the honey and dried chilli flakes.

5 Once bubbling again, add the fried chicken mini fillets to the pan with the chopped spring onion greens, and stir in. Continue to allow the mixture to bubble until it reduces a little and looks lovely and sticky.

6 Finish with a sprinkle of dried chilli flakes and serve immediately while the chicken is still nice and crispy. Serve with a microwavable packet of rice for ease, or pineapple and cashew nut fried rice (page 135) for the ultimate fakeaway experience.

7 Optionally serve with crispy seaweed (page 134), salt and pepper chips (page 138) or veggie spring rolls (page 157).

TIP You can make this recipe even lazier by using store-bought gluten-free tempura chicken and making the sauce to go alongside.

use a thick dairy-free yoghurt/cheese

 use lactose-free Greek yoghurt

 use lactose-free Greek yoghurt and ensure all toppings are FODMAP-friendly

 use a thick dairy-free yoghurt/cheese

- 1 x 125g (4½oz) ball of mozzarella, cut into strips 1.5cm (½in) thick
- 100g (3½oz) extra-mature Cheddar, grated
- 4–5 fresh basil leaves, to serve

For the dough

- 200g (1½ cups) gluten-free self-raising (self-rising) flour
- 205g (7¼oz) Greek yoghurt (or any thick, natural yoghurt)

For the sauce

- 140ml (⅔ cup) passata (sieved tomatoes)
- 1 tsp garlic-infused oil
- 2 tsp dried oregano
- 2 tbsp gluten-free BBQ sauce (optional: for a BBQ base)
- Salt and black pepper

Pictured on page 62

STUFFED CRUST MARGHERITA PIZZA

Makes 1 large pizza ❄
Prep + Cook 30 mins

Finding the phrases 'gluten-free' and 'stuffed-crust pizza' in the same sentence is basically impossible... unless it starts with 'I wish I could eat...'. Fortunately, this is one of the few places on planet Earth that you'll find one and yes, it can also be made in 30 minutes or less. As always, feel free to add your own toppings!

1 Preheat your oven to 240°C fan / 260°C / 500°F, or as hot as it will go.

2 To make the dough, add the flour and yoghurt to a large mixing bowl. Mix thoroughly using a spatula to ensure there are no hidden clumps, then use your hands to bring it together into a slightly sticky ball. Knead the dough briefly in the bowl until smooth, combined and no longer sticky. Dough still too sticky? Add a little more flour to the dough. Dough too dry? Add a little more yoghurt.

3 Transfer the dough to a large sheet of non-stick baking parchment. Lightly flour your rolling pin and roll out the dough to a large, even circle, aiming for a 1mm (½2in) thickness, re-flouring your rolling pin as necessary to stop it from sticking.

4 Place the strips of mozzarella around the edge of the pizza in a circle, leaving a 2.5cm (1in) border around the edge. Brush the dough either side of the mozzarella with water, all around the circle, then carefully fold the dough over the mozzarella and press down to create a ridged crust. Press to completely seal so the mozzarella can't escape.

5 Slide a round pizza tray underneath the pizza and transfer to the oven for 5 minutes. While it's cooking, combine all the ingredients for the sauce in a small bowl, adding salt and pepper to taste.

6 Remove the base from the oven - it should have started to colour slightly on the crust. Spread the sauce over your base, right up to the mozzarella-filled ridge. Add any toppings of your choice, if using, finish with grated Cheddar, then bake in the oven for a further 12 minutes, or until the cheese is nicely browned and golden. Finish with a few fresh basil leaves and optionally serve alongside my cheat's gluten-free garlic bread (page 142).

TIP If using a different type of yoghurt that isn't quite as thick, simply add a little more flour to compensate.

LAZY COMFORT FOOD

This chapter loosely translates as: put in 15 minutes of effort or less, then put your feet up while it cooks. Just remember to set a timer so you don't forget it's cooking!

So though these recipes may take longer than 30 minutes in total, they actually ask for less of your time and effort than some of the other recipes in this book. Trust me, there's nothing more satisfying than knowing a hearty, home-cooked meal is on its way while you're just watching the telly.

Here you'll find my favourite one-tray and one-pot recipes (unintended bonus: they result in so much less washing up) which are the perfect all-in-one meals that are incredibly easy to prepare. Plus, I absolutely had to include all of my slow-cooker stunners, which are the ultimate 'throw it all in and it magically transforms into dinner' meals.

But of course, since this book has the word 'quick' in the title (and I take that very, very seriously, apparently) I've also included instructions on how to make my slow-cooker recipes in a pressure cooker too, which actually reduces the cooking time down to less than 30 minutes.

Or, if you don't even own a slow cooker or pressure cooker, I've thrown in instructions on how to cook them in the oven as well, because I'm nice like that.

Welcome to lazy comfort food heaven, where everything is gluten-free!

use gluten-free veggie/vegan stock, omit the lamb and use the entire can of chickpeas

 follow the vegetarian advice above

- 250-300g (9-10½oz) lamb neck fillets, chopped into strips 1cm (½in) thick
- 1 tbsp garlic-infused oil, plus extra to serve
- 1 tbsp cornflour (cornstarch)
- 1 onion, finely chopped, or 60g (2oz) leek, finely chopped
- 1 medium carrot, chopped into 1cm (½in) chunks
- 1 tsp ground cumin
- 1 tsp smoked paprika
- 1 tsp ground coriander
- 1 tsp ground cinnamon
- 1 tsp sumac (optional)
- ½ tsp salt
- ½ tsp black pepper
- 100g (3½oz) dried apricots, chopped into quarters
- 1 tbsp minced ginger paste
- ½ x 400g (14oz) can chickpeas, drained and rinsed
- 300ml (1½ cups) hot gluten-free lamb stock
- 200g (7oz) passata (sieved tomatoes)
- Handful of fresh coriander (cilantro), roughly chopped, to serve

ONE-POT LAMB TAGINE

Serves 3 ❄

SC 4 hours / Oven 2 hours / PC 35 mins

While this is far from being cooked in an actual tagine, my one-pot version is fruity, spiced to perfection and packed with chickpeas and chunks of super-tender lamb. Simply serve with rice or a gluten-free pitta.

To cook in a slow cooker

Place everything in the slow cooker apart from the stock, passata and fresh coriander. Mix thoroughly so that everything is well dispersed and, most importantly, that there are no lumps of cornflour. Add the stock and passata, stir briefly and use a wooden spoon to gently compact everything down below the liquid as much as possible. Pop the lid on and cook on low for around 4 hours, or high for 2 hours, or until the carrots are soft in the middle – you can poke them with a skewer to check. For the last 5-15 minutes, cook with the lid removed to allow the stew to thicken up to your liking.

To cook in the oven

Preheat your oven to 140°C fan / 160°C / 325°F.

Place all the ingredients except the coriander in a large, lidded casserole dish. Stir well, then pop the lid on and place in the oven for around 2 hours, or until the carrots are soft in the middle – you can poke them with a skewer to check.

To cook in a pressure cooker

Place all the ingredients except the coriander in the pressure cooker, pop the lid on and cook for 20-25 minutes. Use the quick-release function to release the pressure and with the lid open, set to a sauté setting and cook for a further 5-15 minutes to allow the stew to thicken up to your liking.

To serve, drizzle 1 teaspoon of garlic-infused oil over each serving, top with coriander and serve with rice (or a gluten-free pitta bread).

use dairy-free 'buttery' margarine, cream and a thick dairy-free yoghurt

 use lactose-free Greek yoghurt and cream

 follow the low-lactose advice above, use carrot instead of onion, swap the garlic paste for garlic-infused oil and omit the mango chutney

 use 300g (10½oz) king oyster mushrooms, halved, instead of chicken

 combine the dairy-free and vegetarian advice

- 400g (14oz) boneless, skinless chicken thighs
- 1 tsp minced ginger paste
- 1 tsp minced garlic paste
- 1 onion, finely chopped or 1 medium carrot, chopped into 1cm (½in) chunks
- 3 tbsp tomato purée (paste)
- 2 tbsp butter
- 400ml (1⅔ cups) boiling water
- 2 heaped tbsp Greek yoghurt
- 2 tbsp double (heavy) cream (optional)
- 1 tbsp cornflour (cornstarch), mixed with 2 tbsp water

For the spice blend

- 1 tbsp garam masala
- ½ tsp ground turmeric
- 1 tsp chilli powder
- 1 tsp ground coriander
- 1 tsp lemon juice
- 1 tsp fenugreek leaves
- 1 tsp salt

To serve

- Handful of fresh coriander (cilantro), roughly chopped
- Basmati rice
- Gluten-free naan breads (see page 142 for homemade)
- Mango chutney

LAZY BUTTER CHICKEN CURRY

Serves 3 ❄

SC 4½ hours / **Oven** 2 hours 10 mins / **PC** 30 mins

This one-pot wonder is the zero-effort curry that never fails to please a crowd. Think juicy chunks of chicken coated in a creamy, mildly spiced sauce that's perfect served alongside my speedy naan bread (page 142).

Mix the ingredients for the spice blend together in a small bowl.

To cook in a slow cooker

Place the chicken, ginger, garlic paste, onion or carrot, tomato purée, butter and water in the slow cooker. Stir in the spice blend until everything is combined, ignoring that the butter is still in a lump! Pop the lid on and cook on low for around 4 hours, or high for 2 hours, until the chicken is nicely done. Stir in the yoghurt, cream, if using, and cornflour mixture, then leave the lid off and cook for a further 30 minutes, to allow the sauce to thicken.

To cook in the oven

Preheat your oven to 140°C fan / 160°C / 325°F.

Place the chicken, ginger, garlic paste, onion or carrot, tomato purée, butter and water in a large, lidded and flameproof casserole dish. Stir in the spice blend until everything is combined, ignoring that the butter is still in a lump! Pop the lid on and place in the oven for around 2 hours, or until the chicken is nicely done. Remove the lid, stir in the yoghurt, cream (if using) and cornflour mixture then place on the hob over a medium heat for about 5–10 minutes to allow the sauce to thicken up to your liking.

To cook in a pressure cooker

Follow the instructions for the slow cooker, but cook for 20–25 minutes. Use the quick-release function to release the pressure, stir in the yoghurt, cream, if using, and cornflour mixture. Set to a sauté setting and cook for a further 5–10 minutes.

To serve, sprinkle over the coriander and serve with basmati rice, gluten-free naan breads and mango chutney on the side.

DF

 LF

 F use low FODMAP stock cube and curry powder

 V use a gluten-free veggie/vegan stock cube and 200g (7oz) button mushrooms, halved, instead of chicken or beef

 VE follow the vegetarian advice above

- 400g (14oz) boneless, skinless chicken thighs or beef stewing steak, cut into bite-sized chunks
- 2 medium carrots (about 180g/6½oz), sliced 2cm (¾in) thick
- 40g (1½oz) creamed coconut block
- 1 gluten-free chicken stock cube
- 500ml (generous 2 cups) boiling water
- 4 tbsp frozen peas
- 1½ tbsp cornflour (cornstarch) mixed with 3 tbsp water
- Handful of spring onion (scallion) greens, chopped, to serve

For the curry paste

- 1 tbsp mild curry powder
- 1 tsp dried chilli flakes
- ½ tsp five spice
- 1 tbsp garlic-infused oil
- 1 tbsp gluten-free soy sauce

1-POT CHINESE CHICKEN OR BEEF CURRY

Serves 3 ❄

SC 4 hours **/ Oven** 2 hours 10 mins **/ PC** 30 mins

Meet the 'throw it all in and go about your business' version of the Chinese chicken or beef curry from my first book. Giving this curry time to stew only enhances the flavour tenfold and it requires almost zero effort. Now that's hard to argue with.

In a small bowl, combine all the curry paste ingredients.

To cook in a slow cooker

Place the chicken or beef, carrots, coconut, stock cube and water in the slow cooker, followed by your curry paste. Stir well to combine, ignoring that the coconut is still a solid block! Pop the lid on and cook on low for around 4 hours, or high for 2 hours, or until the carrots are soft in the middle – you can poke them with a skewer to check. About 20 minutes before it's done, stir in the frozen peas and cornflour mixture. Leave the lid off for the remaining time to allow the sauce to thicken.

To cook in the oven

Preheat your oven to 140°C fan / 160°C / 325°F.

Place the chicken or beef, carrots, coconut, stock cube and water in a large, lidded and flameproof casserole dish. Stir well to combine, ignoring that the coconut is still a solid block! Pop the lid on and place in the oven for around 2 hours, or until the carrots are soft in the middle – you can poke them with a skewer to check. After 2 hours, remove the lid, stir in the frozen peas and the cornflour mixture and place on the hob over a medium heat for about 5-10 minutes to allow the sauce to thicken up to your liking.

To cook in a pressure cooker

Follow the instructions for a slow cooker, but cook for 20-25 minutes. Use the quick-release function to release the pressure, then stir in the frozen peas and cornflour mixture. Set to a sauté setting and cook for a further 5-10 minutes to allow the sauce to thicken.

To serve, sprinkle with spring onion greens and serve with my pineapple and cashew nut fried rice (page 135).

TIP Use an extra ½ tablespoon cornflour mixed with 1 tablespoon water if the sauce isn't thick enough for your liking.

For the chicken

- 400g (14oz) boneless, skinless chicken thighs
- 2 tsp smoked paprika
- 2 tsp dried mixed herbs
- 1 tsp sumac (optional)
- ½ tsp salt
- ½ tsp black pepper
- 1 tbsp garlic-infused oil

For the rice

- 200g (7oz) basmati or long-grain rice
- 80g (3oz) leek, finely chopped
- 1 tbsp smoked paprika
- 1 tsp dried mixed herbs
- ½ tsp each of salt and black pepper
- 1 tbsp garlic-infused oil
- 1 yellow (bell) pepper, chopped into 2.5cm (1in) chunks
- 1 x 400g (14oz) can chopped tomatoes
- 500ml (generous 2 cups) hot gluten-free chicken stock

Pictured on page 88

OVEN-BAKED CHICKEN PAPRIKA RICE

Serves 3 ❄

Prep 5 mins **+ Cook** 40 mins

It doesn't get lazier than this, but at the same time, food doesn't really get much better than this either! With a spicy tomato rice and yellow pepper hiding underneath roasted, tender, smoky paprika chicken, it's hard to believe this was all baked in one dish.

1 Preheat your oven to 200°C fan / 220°C / 425°F.

2 Put all the ingredients for the chicken into a large mixing bowl, stir well until the chicken is well coated, then set aside.

3 Put everything for the rice, except the stock, in a large roasting dish (mine is 33 x 20cm/13 x 8 inch) or a large, lidded and flameproof casserole dish. Mix well until everything is evenly dispersed, then add the stock.

4 Place the chicken on top of the rice then tightly cover the roasting dish in foil or place the lid on the casserole dish.

5 Bake in the oven for 25 minutes, then remove the foil or lid and cook for another 15 minutes before tucking in.

MANCHESTER DHAL

Serves 4 ❄

SC 4 hours / **Oven** 2 hours / **PC** 30 mins

- 200g (7oz) dried red lentils (ensure gluten-free; see TIP)
- 2 small sweet potatoes (about 400g/14oz in total), peeled and chopped into 1cm (½in) cubes
- 1 onion, finely diced, or 60g (2oz) leek, finely chopped
- 2 tbsp garlic-infused oil
- 1 x 400g (14oz) can chopped tomatoes
- 1 tbsp minced ginger paste
- 1 tsp minced chilli paste
- 2 tsp ground cumin
- 1 tsp ground coriander
- ½ tsp garam masala
- 1 tsp salt
- ¼ tsp black pepper
- 1 gluten-free vegetable stock cube, crumbled
- 40g (1½oz) creamed coconut block (optional)
- 700ml (3 cups) boiling water
- Handful of fresh coriander (cilantro), roughly chopped, to serve

I realize that Manchester isn't a city that's famous for its dhal. However, it is the place where I first tried it many years ago, in a little café hidden underneath our favourite vegan supermarket. Since Mark and I moved away from Manchester, I've created my own version to satisfy my cravings - it is thick and creamy, mildly spicy and packed with a warming, cosy blend of spices.

To cook in a slow cooker

Place all the ingredients except the water and fresh coriander in the slow cooker. Mix thoroughly so everything is well dispersed (ignoring that the coconut, if using, is still a solid block), then add the water. Stir briefly and use a wooden spoon to gently compact everything down below the water as much as possible. Pop the lid on and cook on low for around 4 hours, or high for 2 hours. For the last 10-20 minutes, cook with the lid removed to allow it to thicken up to your liking.

To cook in the oven

Preheat your oven to 140°C fan / 160°C / 325°F.

Place all the ingredients except the fresh coriander in a large, lidded casserole dish, pop the lid on and place in the oven for around 2 hours until thick and creamy.

To cook in a pressure cooker

Place all the ingredients except the fresh coriander in the pressure cooker, pop the lid on and cook for 20-25 minutes. Use the quick-release function to release the pressure and, with the lid open, set to a sauté setting and cook for a further 5-10 minutes to allow it to thicken up to your liking.

Serve topped with fresh coriander, alongside rice and/or my speedy naan (page 142).

TIP Dried lentils often have a 'may contain' warning for wheat or gluten due to cross-contamination during manufacturing processes. If you can't find gluten-free dried lentils, then try canned lentils instead - they're usually less likely to have a 'may contain' warning. Drain the can well and reduce the water quantity in the recipe by half.

use a low FODMAP stock cube, use leek (green parts only) instead of onion, and use garlic-infused oil instead of garlic paste

use a gluten-free veggie/vegan stock cube, use 200g (7oz) button mushrooms (halved) instead of chicken or beef, and omit the Worcestershire sauce

For the stew

- 400g (14oz) boneless, skinless chicken thighs or beef stewing steak, diced
- 1 onion, finely diced or 60g (2oz) leek, finely chopped
- 1 medium potato, cut into bite-sized chunks
- 1 medium carrot, sliced 1cm (½in) thick
- 2 celery sticks, chopped
- 1 tsp garlic-infused oil or minced garlic paste
- 1 bay leaf
- 1 tsp dried rosemary
- 1 tsp smoked paprika
- ½ tsp gluten-free Worcestershire sauce
- ¼ tsp gluten-free gravy browning sauce (optional)
- ½ tsp salt
- ¼ tsp black pepper
- 2 tbsp gluten-free plain (all-purpose) flour
- ½ gluten-free chicken or beef stock cube, crumbled
- 400ml (1⅔ cups) boiling water

For the puff pastry stars

- 280g (10oz) store-bought gluten-free puff pastry
- 1 egg, beaten

BEEF OR CHICKEN STEW WITH PUFF PASTRY STARS

Serves 3

SC 4 hours / **Oven** 2½ hours / **PC** 30 mins

Here's a classic stew that simply involves throwing everything into a big pot, covering and cooking. For the ultimate experience, serve up in one my XL gluten-free Yorkshire puddings (page 143).

Place all the stew ingredients except the water in a slow cooker, large, lidded and flameproof casserole dish or a pressure cooker. Mix thoroughly so that everything is well dispersed and there are no lumps of flour. Add the water and stir briefly, then use a wooden spoon to gently compact everything down below the water as much as possible.

To cook in a slow cooker

Pop the lid on and cook on low for around 4 hours, high for 2 hours, or until the carrots are soft in the middle - you can poke them with a skewer to check. Remove the lid for the last 30 minutes to allow the stew to thicken up to your liking.

To cook in the oven

Preheat the oven to 140°C fan / 160°C / 325°F. Pop a lid on the casserole dish and place in the oven for 2-2½ hours, or until the carrots are soft in the middle - you can poke them with a skewer to check. Remove the lid and place on the hob over a medium heat for about 5-10 minutes to allow the stew to thicken up to your liking.

To cook in a pressure cooker

Pop the lid on and cook for 20-25 minutes. Use the quick-release function to release the pressure and, with the lid open, set to a sauté setting and cook for a further 5-15 minutes to allow the stew to thicken.

For the puff pastry stars

Preheat your oven to 200°C fan / 220°C / 425°F and line two baking sheets with non-stick baking parchment. Unroll the pastry on a work surface. Use a 5cm (2in) star cookie cutter to cut out as many stars as you can, then transfer them to the baking sheet. Brush the stars with beaten egg and bake for 10 minutes, or until slightly puffy and golden. Plate up the stew with the puff pastry stars on top.

use a dairy-free cheese that melts well

 omit the tuna

 omit the tuna and use a dairy-free cheese

- 190g (6¾oz) dried gluten-free pasta
- 1 x 145g (5oz) can of tuna chunks
- ½ courgette (zucchini), chopped into 1cm (½in) cubes
- ½ yellow (bell) pepper, chopped into 1.5cm (¾in) chunks
- ½ small aubergine (eggplant), chopped into 1cm (½in) cubes
- Small handful of spring onion (scallion) greens, finely chopped
- 400ml (1⅔ cups) good-quality passata (sieved tomatoes) or 1 x 400g (14oz) canned chopped tomatoes
- 1 tbsp red wine vinegar or cider vinegar
- 3 tbsp garlic-infused oil
- 1 tsp salt
- ½ tsp black pepper
- 400ml (1⅔ cups) boiling water
- 100g (3½oz) mozzarella, grated or shredded

RATATOUILLE TUNA PASTA BAKE

Serves 3 ❄

Prep 5 mins **+ Cook** 40 mins

There aren't many meals that only take 5 minutes of prep, but this is one of them - it's an absolute lifesaver when we want a comforting meal, but can't be bothered to cook. The top is crisp and super-cheesy, with perfectly cooked pasta, courgette (zucchini), flaky tuna and a creamy tomato sauce hiding beneath. Just bung everything into a roasting dish and bake!

1 Preheat your oven to 200°C fan / 220°C / 425°F.

2 Put all the ingredients apart from the boiling water and mozzarella in a 20 x 33cm (8 x 13in) roasting dish. Give it all a good stir until everything is evenly dispersed. Add the boiling water and gently press everything down with a large spoon so that it's below the water as much as possible, especially the pasta.

3 Place the roasting dish into the oven for 30 minutes. After 30 minutes, top with the mozzarella and place back in the oven for a further 10 minutes, or until the mozzarella is melted and golden brown on top.

4 Serve with fresh rocket (arugula) and my cheat's garlic bread (page 142).

TIP If using a smaller roasting dish, cook it for 5 minutes longer. Chopping your veg into small cubes ensures they're well cooked, so no big, huge chunks please! Don't like tuna? Feel free to leave it out and proceed with the recipe as directed.

use a low FODMAP BBQ sauce

- 1 tsp garlic-infused oil
- 700g (1lb 8½oz) pork ribs, separated between the bone
- 200ml (generous ¾ cup) gluten-free BBQ sauce
- Spring onion (scallion) greens, finely chopped (optional)

3-INGREDIENT STICKY BBQ RIBS

Serves 3–4 ❄

SC 4 hours / Oven 2 hours / PC 25 mins

I've had so many requests for BBQ ribs over the years, so here it is! I bet you didn't expect it to be so simple, right? Your average BBQ sauce has everything in it, from sugar, to spices and even thickener that turns it into a sticky coating once cooked - just ensure your BBQ sauce is gluten-free before you start!

To cook in a slow cooker

Add the garlic-infused oil to the slow cooker and use a brush or kitchen paper to lightly grease the base. Add the ribs, followed by the BBQ sauce, and mix until well coated. Pop the lid on and cook on low for around 4 hours or high for 2 hours. To finish, transfer the ribs and any remaining juices left in the slow cooker to a large saucepan. Place over a medium heat for 7–8 minutes, stirring occasionally while it's nicely bubbling, until the ribs are coated in a thick, sticky sauce.

To cook in the oven

Preheat your oven to 140°C fan / 160°C / 325°F.

Add the garlic-infused oil to a large, lidded and flameproof casserole dish and use a brush or kitchen paper to lightly grease the base. Add the ribs, followed by the BBQ sauce, and mix until well coated. Pop the lid on and place in the oven for around 2 hours. To finish, place the casserole dish, uncovered, over a medium heat on the hob for 7-8 minutes. Stir occasionally and ensure it's nicely bubbling until the ribs are coated in a thick, sticky sauce.

To cook in a pressure cooker

Add the garlic-infused oil to the slow cooker and use a brush or kitchen paper to lightly grease the base. Add the ribs, followed by the BBQ sauce, and mix until well coated. Pop the lid on and cook for 15 minutes. Use the quick-release function to release the pressure and, with the lid open, set to a sauté setting and cook for a further 10 minutes until the ribs are coated in a thick, sticky sauce.

To serve, transfer the ribs to a serving plate, sprinkle with spring onion greens, if using, and enjoy.

use dairy-free 'buttery' margarine

 use leek instead of onion (green parts only), low FODMAP stock and omit the mushrooms

 use dairy-free 'buttery' margarine, veggie/vegan stock and a veggie/vegan meat-free mince

 follow the vegetarian advice and use dairy-free milk to brush the pie dish and pastry

---

- 2 tbsp garlic-infused oil
- 400g (14oz) beef mince (ground beef)
- 1 tbsp butter
- ½ onion, finely diced or 80g (3oz) leek, chopped
- 1 medium carrot, cut into 1cm (½in) cubes
- 100g (3½oz) button mushrooms, thinly sliced
- 2 tbsp cornflour (cornstarch)
- 200ml (generous ¾ cup) gluten-free beef stock
- 200ml (generous ¾ cup) gluten-free pale ale (or use more beef stock)
- ½ tsp gluten-free gravy browning sauce (optional)
- Pinch each of salt and black pepper
- 1 tbsp dried thyme
- 1 egg, beaten
- 280g (10oz) store-bought gluten-free puff pastry (see TIP if using homemade)

PUFF PASTRY BEEF AND ALE PIE

Serves 3-4 ❊
Prep 20 mins **+ Cook** 20 mins

When the rest of the world uses store-bought puff pastry for convenient, quick, comforting food, why can't we? This hearty beef pie is a hug in a roasting dish, topped with perfectly cooked crisp, flaky pastry which, if you follow my cooking method, will puff up beautifully and taste wonderful. Of course, you can always make your own pastry for this if you have time – see the tips below.

1 Place a large frying pan over a medium heat and add the garlic-infused oil. Once hot, add the beef mince and fry, stirring, until lightly browned, then remove from the pan.

2 Add the butter to the pan and, once melted, add the onion or leek, carrot and mushrooms. Fry until the mushrooms are a little golden, then return the cooked beef back to the pan. Add the cornflour and stir until everything is evenly coated, then add the stock, ale, gravy browning, if using, salt, pepper and dried thyme. Bring to the boil and simmer for 8-10 minutes, or until the sauce is thickened to a gravy-like consistency. Meanwhile, preheat your oven to 200°C fan / 220°C / 425°F.

3 Transfer the pie filling to a 20cm (8in) round pie dish and brush the edges of the dish with beaten egg. Lay the sheet of puff pastry over it and trim around the edge, leaving around a 5mm (¼in) overhang around the edges of the dish. Tuck the overhang underneath the rim of the pie dish and place on a baking sheet.

4 Brush the pastry with beaten egg, make a couple of holes in the top using a small knife, then bake for 10 minutes until the pastry is lovely and golden. Cover loosely with foil and bake for a further 10 minutes.

TIP The store-bought gluten-free pastry I use (see page 12 for the specific brand) gets very overdone and crispy unless covered with foil, so this step is essential. If using homemade pastry I'd highly recommend making my gluten-free rough puff pastry from either my first or second book; you'll likely only need to cover it with foil for the last 5 minutes of cooking time. You could also make my ultimate shortcrust pastry recipe on page 194. To make three small pies instead of one big one, use three 12cm (5in) individual round pie dishes and cut out 3 circles from the pastry, following the directions for assembling and cooking times as given for creamy chicken and mushroom pot pies on page 106.

- Vegetable oil, for greasing
- 4 chicken thighs, bone in, skin on
- 1 tsp dried rosemary
- 2 medium carrots
- 2 medium parsnips
- 2 tbsp maple syrup
- Salt and black pepper

For the smashed potatoes

- 10 new potatoes, cleaned
- 2 tbsp vegetable oil
- 1 tbsp dried rosemary

ONE-TRAY CHICKEN ROAST DINNER WITH SMASHED POTATOES

Serves 2

Prep 10 mins **+ Cook** 40 mins

When I think of a roast dinner, I also think of millions of pots on the go at once. But with my cheat's chicken roast dinner, all you need to do is throw all the raw ingredients onto a tray, then put your feet up. And perhaps better still, there will be barely any washing up to do after!

1 Preheat your oven to 180°C fan / 200°C / 400°F. Lightly grease a large baking tray with vegetable oil, then place your chicken thighs on it – spread them out, leaving equal gaps between them. Season with salt, pepper and the dried rosemary. Turn the thighs over a few times to ensure they get a light coating of oil, leaving them skin-side up.

2 Put the potatoes in a large mixing bowl with the vegetable oil, dried rosemary and salt to taste. Mix thoroughly until well coated, then transfer to the baking tray, tucking them in between the chicken thighs.

3 Prepare your carrots and parsnips by peeling them, halving them (lengthways) then cutting in half again. Place in the empty mixing bowl (no need to clean it), add the maple syrup, then mix until well coated. Transfer to the baking tray so that everything fits in a single layer.

4 Bake in the oven for 30 minutes, then remove from the oven and push down on top of each potato, using a potato masher, until it splits. Place back in the oven for another 20 minutes, or until the chicken skin is crispy and golden.

5 Enjoy with lots of gluten-free gravy and, if you have a little extra time, serve up in one of my XL gluten-free Yorkshire puddings (page 143).

use a low FODMAP hot sauce
and maple syrup instead of
honey

- 1kg (2lb 4oz) chicken wings, halved at the joint (see TIP)
- 1 tbsp cornflour (cornstarch)
- 100ml (scant ½ cup) buffalo hot sauce (ensure gluten-free)
- 100ml (scant ½ cup) honey
- 1 tsp Italian seasoning or dried mixed herbs
- Salt and black pepper, to taste

5-INGREDIENT HONEY BUFFALO WINGS

Serves 3-4 ❄

SC 4 hours / **Oven** 2 hours 10 mins / **PC** 25 mins

Nothing beats sweet, sticky and spicy chicken wings, especially when they're so dangerously simple to make!

To cook in a slow cooker

Add the chicken to the slow cooker, followed by the cornflour. Mix until well coated, then stir in all the remaining ingredients. Pop the lid on and cook on low for around 4 hours, or high for 2 hours. To finish, transfer the wings and any remaining juices to a large saucepan. Place over a medium heat and bring to a rapid bubble for 8-9 minutes, stirring gently only once or twice; don't stir it too often or the meat will fall off the bone! They are ready when you're left with a lovely sticky coating.

To cook in the oven

Preheat your oven to 140°C fan / 160°C / 325°F.

Add the chicken wings to a large, lidded and flameproof casserole dish, followed by the cornflour. Mix until well coated, then stir in all the remaining ingredients. Pop the lid on and place in the oven for around 2 hours. To finish, place the casserole dish onto the hob (lid off) over a medium heat and bring to a rapid bubble for 8-9 minutes, stirring gently only once or twice; don't stir it too often or the meat will fall off the bone! They are ready when you're left with a lovely sticky coating.

To cook in a pressure cooker

Add the chicken wings to the pressure cooker, followed by the cornflour. Mix until well coated, then stir in all the remaining ingredients. Pop the lid on and cook for 15 minutes. Use the quick-release function to release the pressure and, with the lid open, set to a sauté setting and bring to a rapid bubble for 8-9 minutes, stirring gently only once or twice; don't stir it too often or the meat will fall off the bone! They are done when you're left with a lovely sticky coating.

To serve, carefully transfer the buffalo wings to a large plate and serve alongside a blue cheese dip.

TIP If your chicken wings haven't been halved already, take a sharp knife (or ideally a meat cleaver) and cut the chicken wings in half at the joint. This will create a mini drumstick and a remaining flap piece.

use dairy-free milk and 'buttery' margarine, and omit the cream cheese

 use lactose-free milk and cream cheese

 use veggie/vegan stock and canned lentils (drained) instead of chicken, adding them with the stock

 combine the dairy-free and vegetarian advice and use dairy-free milk to brush the pie dish and pastry

---

- 2 tbsp garlic-infused oil
- 400g (14oz) boneless, skinless chicken thighs, chopped into bite-sized chunks
- 1 tbsp butter
- ½ onion, finely diced or 80g (3oz) leek, chopped
- 200g (7oz) button mushrooms, thinly sliced
- 2 tbsp cornflour (cornstarch)
- 250ml (1 cup) gluten-free chicken stock
- 150ml (⅝ cup) milk
- Pinch each of salt and black or white pepper
- 1 tbsp dried thyme
- 1 tbsp cream cheese (optional)
- 280g (10oz) store-bought gluten-free puff pastry (see TIP if using homemade)
- 1 egg, beaten

CREAMY CHICKEN AND MUSHROOM POT PIES

Serves 3-4 ❄

Prep 20 mins + Cook 15 mins

Store-bought gluten-free puff pastry makes another cameo here to top three single serve mini pot pies. If you'd like to make one large pie, see the method for assembling my beef and ale pie on page 102.

1 Place a large frying pan over a medium heat and add the garlic-infused oil. Once hot, fry the chicken until sealed, then remove from the pan.

2 Add the butter to the pan and, once melted, add the onion or leek and mushrooms. Fry until the mushrooms are a little golden, then return the chicken to the pan. Stir in the cornflour, then add the stock, milk, salt and pepper, followed by the dried thyme. Bring to the boil then turn down and simmer for 8-10 minutes, or until the sauce is thickened to a gravy-like consistency. Stir through the cream cheese, if using. Meanwhile, preheat your oven to 200°C fan / 220°C / 425°F.

3 Unroll the puff pastry on a work surface. Arrange three 12cm (5in) pie dishes upside down on top of the pastry and use them as a guide to cut out three large circles 5mm (¼in) larger than the dishes.

4 Divide the pie filling between the dishes, ensuring the filling comes to around 1cm (½in) below the tops. Brush the edges of the dishes with beaten egg. Place the three circles of pastry on top of the dishes and tuck the overhang underneath the rim of the pie dish. Place all three dishes on a baking sheet.

5 Brush the pastry with beaten egg, make a hole in the top of each using a small knife, then bake for 10 minutes until the pastry is golden. Cover loosely with foil and bake for a further 5 minutes.

TIP The store-bought gluten-free pastry I use (see page 12 for the specific brand) gets very overdone and crispy unless covered with foil, so this step is essential. If using homemade pastry I'd recommend making my gluten-free rough puff pastry from either my first or second book; you'll likely only need to cover it with foil for the last 5 minutes of cooking time. You could also make my ultimate shortcrust pastry recipe on page 194.

use dairy-free milk

 use lactose-free milk

 use lactose-free milk and ensure sausages are low FODMAP

 use veggie-friendly, gluten-free sausages

- 1 tbsp vegetable oil
- 6 gluten-free sausages
- 100g (⅘ cup) cornflour (cornstarch)
- ½ tbsp dried rosemary (optional)
- 3 medium eggs
- 150ml (⅝ cup) milk

4-INGREDIENT TOAD IN THE HOLE

Serves 3-4

Prep 5 mins **+ Cook** 35 mins

What do you get when you cross sausages with a Yorkshire pudding? A toad in the hole, of course! This classic can be thrown together using just four ingredients and a smidge of oil and nobody would ever notice it's gluten-free. This one is a tried-and-tested blog favourite that never fails, according to you lovely lot.

1 Preheat your oven to 200°C fan / 220°C / 425°F and add the oil to a 20 x 30cm (8 x 12in) roasting dish. Arrange the sausages in the dish and place into the oven for 10 minutes until showing very slight signs of browning.

2 Meanwhile, in a large mixing bowl, combine the cornflour, rosemary and eggs. Whisk together until smooth, then add half the milk and whisk until smooth and lump-free. Whisk in the remaining milk.

3 Remove the roasting dish from the oven, quickly pour the batter over the top of the sausages and immediately return to the oven.

4 Cook for about 25 minutes until the sausages have browned and the batter is crispy, golden and risen. And please don't open the oven during cooking to check on it, as this will cause it to instantly deflate!

5 Serve with mashed potato, veggies and lots of gluten-free gravy.

WEEKNIGHT FAVOURITES

Welcome to my personal 'greatest hits' chapter of all the everyday meals we make for dinner at home. Over months and years of dinners, these are the recipes that Mark and I find ourselves going back to without fail.

It's a compilation of all the flavours we've fallen in love with on our travels, as well as nostalgic British favourites from closer to home and even re-creations of old-school convenience food that I've missed out on for over a decade.

I think it's safe to say that there's absolutely zero chance we'd ever be able to find any of these in the supermarket or on a gluten-free menu in a restaurant. However, you can easily make them at home in your own kitchen! And best of all, they can all be made in <u>30 minutes or less</u>.

I hope these become part of your meal plans for years to come, just like they have for us.

STICKY JERK-STYLE CHICKEN

Serves 3 ✳

Prep + Cook 25 mins

Mark and I once made dinner using a jar of jerk sauce that was so spicy we couldn't taste anything for the next week (this may be a slight over-exaggeration). Ever since then, we've been making our own version that's a little more kind to the tongue but just as sweet, sticky and flavourful. We usually opt for a mild spice these days, but feel free to double the dried chilli flakes for a medium-hot finish.

- 2 tbsp garlic-infused oil
- 1 red (bell) pepper, cut into 2.5cm (1in) chunks
- 400g (14oz) chicken breast fillet, cut into 2.5cm (1in) chunks
- 2 tsp minced ginger paste
- 200ml (generous ¾ cup) passata (sieved tomatoes)
- 200ml (generous ¾ cup) boiling water
- 4 tbsp gluten-free soy sauce
- 70ml (generous ¼ cup) honey
- 3 tbsp cider vinegar
- 2 tbsp cornflour (cornstarch), mixed with 5 tbsp water
- 1 tsp salt
- Pinch of black pepper
- Handful of spring onion (scallion) greens, finely chopped

For the jerk spice blend
- ½ tsp dried chilli flakes, plus extra to finish
- ½ tsp five spice
- ½ tsp dried thyme
- ½ tsp grated nutmeg
- 1 tsp ground allspice
- 1 tsp onion powder (optional)

1 Combine the spice blend in a small dish and set aside.

2 Place a large pan over a medium heat and add the garlic-infused oil. When hot, add the red pepper to the pan and fry for 2 minutes until slightly softened, then add the chicken and ginger paste and fry for a further minute. Add the spice blend and fry until the chicken is sealed.

3 Add the passata, followed by the boiling water, and mix in well. Add the soy sauce, honey and vinegar and bring to the boil, then reduce to a simmer. Allow to bubble for 8–10 minutes before adding in the cornflour mixture and immediately stirring it in.

4 Season with the salt and pepper, top with spring onion greens and serve with rice.

use a block of halloumi (sliced into strips) instead of cod fillets

---

- 5 tbsp cornflour (cornstarch)
- 1 tsp salt
- ½ tsp white or black pepper
- 2 medium eggs
- 140g (5oz) gluten-free cornflakes
- 2 skinless cod fillets (not too chunky)
- Vegetable oil, for frying

4-INGREDIENT CORNFLAKE-CRUSTED COD GOUJONS

Serves 2–3

Prep + Cook 20 mins

Yep, you can make super-crunchy, golden fish goujons using just cornflour (cornstarch), eggs, cornflakes and cod. Why cornflakes? Well, as corn is a hard grain, it makes the coating super-crunchy when fried – even more so than if you used batter or breadcrumbs!

1 Mix the cornflour, salt and pepper together well and spread out on a large dinner plate. Beat the eggs in a medium bowl. Tip the cornflakes into a large bowl, then use both hands to crush them for 30 seconds; ensure there are no whole cornflakes left or they won't stick to the fish!

2 Slice the cod fillets into strips that are 2.5cm (1in) wide and 10cm (4in) long. Dredge half of the fish in the cornflour until evenly dusted on all sides, then dip them into the egg until well coated. Finally, dredge in the cornflakes, gently compacting the cornflakes onto the fish.

3 Pour oil into a large frying pan to a 5mm (¼in) depth. Place over a medium heat for 5 minutes, or until it reaches 180°C (350°F). If you don't have a digital food thermometer, use the wooden spoon handle test (page 16). Line a large plate with kitchen paper, ready for later.

4 Once the oil is hot, carefully lower all the coated fish strips into the oil using a pair of tongs – they should sizzle nicely. Cook for 5–6 minutes, turning halfway – the coating should be golden brown. While they are cooking, coat the remaining fish strips, ready to fry. Remove the fried goujons using a slotted spoon and place on the plate lined with kitchen paper to absorb excess oil. Repeat the frying process for the rest of your goujons.

5 Serve with chips (page 139), tartare sauce and mushy peas, or chop into chunks and serve in gluten-free crunchy tacos with smashed avocado, sweetcorn and chilli jam.

To cook in an air fryer

Preheat the air fryer to 200°C / 400°F and spray a little oil into the tray. Place as many coated fish strips into the air fryer basket as will fit without touching, then generously spray with oil. Cook for 5–6 minutes, then turn, spray generously with oil once more and cook for a further 4–5 minutes.

use dairy-free milk and use 2 tbsp dairy-free cream instead of cream cheese

 use lactose-free milk and cream cheese

 use lactose-free milk and cream cheese, use maple syrup instead of honey, use the green parts of the leeks only, and use a low FODMAP stock

 use 200g (7oz) button mushrooms (halved) instead of chicken, a large handful of spinach instead of ham, and use vegan/veggie stock

 combine the dairy-free and vegetarian advice and use maple syrup instead of honey

---

- 1 tbsp garlic-infused oil
- 400g (14oz) chicken breast fillet, cut into bite-sized pieces
- 90g (3¼oz) leek, finely chopped
- 2 tbsp cornflour (cornstarch)
- 200ml (generous ¾ cup) gluten-free chicken or ham stock
- 200ml (generous ¾ cup) milk
- Pinch each of salt and black or white pepper
- 3 tbsp frozen peas
- 1 tbsp dried thyme
- 2 tsp Dijon mustard
- 1 tbsp honey
- 4 tbsp cream cheese
- 3 thin slices of ham (about 60g/2oz in total), cut into 2.5cm (1in) strips

CREAMY HONEY MUSTARD CHICKEN WITH HAM

Serves 2–3 ❉
Prep + Cook 20 mins

Meet the meal that makes cooking from scratch an absolute doddle. The sauce is creamy, with the subtle taste of honey, a little kick of mustard and a rich cream cheese finish.

1 Place a large frying pan over a medium heat and add the garlic-infused oil. Once hot, add the chicken and leek, then fry, stirring, until the chicken is sealed. Add the cornflour and stir in until everything is evenly coated, then add the stock, milk, salt and pepper, frozen peas and thyme.

2 Bring to the boil, then reduce to a simmer for 8–10 minutes, or until the sauce is thickened to a gravy-like consistency. Turn the heat down to low, add the mustard, honey, cream cheese and ham, and stir until well combined.

3 Serve with rice or mashed potatoes alongside your choice of steamed veg.

use 2 tbsp dairy-free cream instead of cream cheese

 use lactose-free cream cheese

- 2 tbsp garlic-infused oil
- 400g (14oz) chicken breast fillet, chopped into 2.5cm (1in) chunks
- 1 red (bell) pepper, chopped into 2.5cm (1in) chunks
- 1 x 400g (14oz) can chopped tomatoes
- 400ml (1⅔ cups) gluten-free chicken stock
- 200g (7oz) gluten-free dried pasta
- 3 tbsp cream cheese
- Handful of spring onion (scallion) greens, chopped

For the Cajun spice blend

- 2 tsp smoked paprika
- ½ tsp dried chilli flakes (optional)
- ½ tsp ground cumin
- 2 tsp dried oregano or mixed herbs
- Pinch of cayenne pepper
- 1 tsp salt
- 1 tbsp cornflour (cornstarch)

ONE-POT CREAMY CAJUN CHICKEN PASTA

Serves 2-3 ❄

Prep + Cook 25 mins

In case you hadn't noticed already, I'm very averse to dinners that result in a mountain of washing up; so if you're feeling the same, then I'm dedicating this recipe to you! Who'd have thought you could cook spicy Cajun pasta in a smoky, creamy sauce with chicken all in the same pan?

1 Place a large, lidded saucepan or flameproof casserole dish over a medium heat and add the garlic-infused oil.

2 Put the chicken and the ingredients for the spice blend in a bowl and mix until well coated. Once the oil is hot, add the chicken to the pan and fry for 2 minutes before adding the red pepper.

3 Fry the pepper until slightly softened, then add the chopped tomatoes, stock and pasta. Bring to the boil, then bring down to a simmer and pop the lid on. Cook for 10-15 minutes, or until the liquid has reduced to a sauce-like consistency and the pasta is completely cooked.

4 Remove the lid and turn off the heat. After 1-2 minutes of cooling, stir in the cream cheese until combined before topping with chopped spring onion greens.

TIP You can speed up this recipe even more by using a Cajun spice blend from the supermarket – just use 3 teaspoons of it instead. Don't forget to add the cornflour, however!

HUNTER'S CHICKEN PASTA

Serves 3 ❄

Prep + Cook 25 mins

DF use dairy-free milk, a smoked dairy-free cheese and a 'buttery' margarine

LL use lactose-free milk

F use lactose-free milk and low-FODMAP BBQ sauce

V omit the chicken and bacon and replace with 200g (7oz) steamed broccoli

VE combine the dairy-free and vegetarian advice

- 200g (7oz) gluten-free dried macaroni
- 2 chicken breast fillets (about 400g/14oz in total)
- 8 slices of smoked bacon
- 2 tbsp butter
- 1 tbsp gluten-free plain (all-purpose) flour
- 200ml (¾ cup plus 1½ tbsp) milk
- 150g (5oz) extra-mature Cheddar, grated
- ½ tsp salt
- ¼ tsp white pepper
- 1 tbsp gluten-free BBQ sauce, plus extra to serve
- Handful of spring onion (scallion) greens, finely chopped
- 3 handfuls of rocket (arugula), to serve

This is classic pub food at its best, which when combined with a super-duper-easy-peasy mac and cheese, makes an easy all-in-one meal that you'd never believe took less than 30 minutes.

1 Preheat your oven to 200°C fan / 220°C / 425°F.

2 Cook the macaroni in a saucepan of boiling, salted water according to the packet instructions. Gluten-free pasta can often clump together, but adding it straight into boiling water with 1 teaspoon of oil can massively help to prevent this.

3 Meanwhile, slice each chicken breast fillet in half lengthways. Wrap each portion in 2 slices of bacon. Place on a baking sheet and bake in the oven for 18–20 minutes.

4 While the chicken is baking, make the sauce. Place a large frying pan over a medium heat and add the butter. Once melted, add the flour and stir until it forms a smooth, lump-free paste. Pour in the milk and stir until it turns into a smooth sauce, then remove from the heat. Add the grated cheese and mix until it all melts in. Season with the salt and pepper, and mix in the BBQ sauce.

5 Drain the macaroni and add to the pan. Mix until well coated in the sauce.

6 By now, the chicken should be done; if so, remove from the oven and transfer to a chopping board. Slice into bite-sized pieces.

7 To serve, plate up the macaroni, top with the sliced chicken, drizzle extra BBQ sauce on top, and finish each serving with spring onion greens and a handful of rocket.

use lactose-free cream cheese

 use lactose-free cream cheese

 use extra-mature Cheddar instead of Parmesan

- ½ small head of broccoli (about 100g/3½oz), broken into florets and cut into bite-sized chunks
- 200g (7oz) gluten-free dried spaghetti or penne
- 2 tbsp garlic-infused oil
- 120g (scant ½ cup) cream cheese
- 30g (1oz) Parmesan, grated, plus extra to serve
- ½ tsp each of salt and black pepper
- ¼ tsp dried chilli flakes (optional)

BROCCOLI AND CHEESE PASTA IN SAUCE

Serves 2–3

Prep + Cook 15 mins

This is a great example of why it's getting a little awkward on the rare occasions I'm interviewed and inevitably asked: 'What inspires you when creating recipes?' This recipe was inspired by something I haven't eaten in years: a sachet of pasta with dried broccoli and powdered cheese that just requires adding boiling water. Not exactly gourmet food is it?! Granted, mine is a lot fresher, cheesier and a million miles less processed, but the inspiration remains the same!

1 Boil a kettle then place a large saucepan over a medium heat. Add the broccoli to the pan and fill just over halfway with boiling water. Bring to the boil and cook for 4–5 minutes before removing with a slotted spoon and transferring to a bowl. Add the pasta to the boiling broccoli water and cook according to the packet instructions.

2 Meanwhile, place a large frying pan over a low heat and add the garlic-infused oil, cream cheese, Parmesan, salt and pepper. Stir until melted, then turn off the heat.

3 Once the pasta is done, drain and add straight into the frying pan. Stir until well coated in the sauce, then add the cooked broccoli and briefly stir in.

4 Sprinkle with chilli flakes, if using, and extra Parmesan, and serve alongside a generous handful of rocket (arugula) and my cheat's garlic bread (page 142).

use a dairy-free cheese that melts well and use dairy-free pesto

 swap the tuna for 1 medium courgette (zucchini), chopped into 1cm (½in) cubes, adding them with the (bell) pepper and cherry tomatoes, and ensure the pesto is veggie/vegan-friendly

 combine the dairy-free and vegetarian advice

- 1 tbsp garlic-infused oil
- 1 red (bell) pepper, chopped into 2.5cm (1in) chunks
- 7–8 cherry tomatoes, halved
- 500g (1lb 2oz) gluten-free gnocchi
- 3 heaped tbsp pesto
- ½ tsp salt
- ¼ tsp black pepper
- 1 x 145g (5oz) can tuna, drained
- Handful of gluten-free breadcrumbs
- 1 x 125g (4½oz) mozzarella ball (or buffalo mozzarella), torn into pieces

TUNA, PESTO AND MOZZARELLA GNOCCHI BAKE

Serves 3 ❄
Prep + Cook 20 mins

Gluten-free gnocchi has been available in gluten-free/'free from' sections in supermarkets for years, but nobody ever seems to know what to do with it. So here's a super-simple idea that makes use of canned tuna and a jar of pesto. When paired with cherry tomatoes, mozzarella and a few finishing touches, gnocchi will soon be part of your weekly meal plans.

1 Preheat your oven to 200°C fan / 220°C / 425°F.

2 Add the garlic-infused oil to a large ovenproof frying pan or skillet. Once hot, add the red pepper and cherry tomatoes and fry for 1 minute. Add the gnocchi and fry, stirring occasionally, until a little golden brown and crispy in places.

3 Next add the pesto, salt and pepper and drained tuna. Mix in thoroughly until everything is evenly coated in pesto. Next, flatten everything down into one even layer.

4 Top with the breadcrumbs and mozzarella and bake in the oven for 10–12 minutes, or until the cheese is golden brown and the breadcrumbs are crisp.

TIP If you don't own an ovenproof frying pan or skillet, simply transfer the mixture to a roasting dish before adding the breadcrumbs and mozzarella. You can also make this recipe using your own homemade gluten-free gnocchi – you'll find the recipe in my first book *How To Make Anything Gluten Free*.

use a dairy-free 'buttery' margarine and dairy-free cream

 use lactose-free cream

 use low FODMAP stock, lactose-free cream and omit the mushrooms

 use veggie/vegan stock and a veggie/vegan mince

 combine the vegetarian and dairy-free advice and omit the egg from the meatballs

---

- Vegetable oil, for greasing
- Cranberry sauce, to serve
- Mashed potatoes, to serve

For the meatballs

- 50g (1¾oz) gluten-free breadcrumbs
- 250g (9oz) beef mince (ground beef)
- 150g (5oz) pork mince (ground pork), or use more beef mince
- 1 medium egg
- ½ tsp ground allspice
- ½ tsp salt
- ½ tsp black or white pepper
- 1 tbsp garlic-infused oil

For the sauce

- 1 tbsp garlic-infused oil
- 2 tbsp butter
- 100g (3½oz) button mushrooms, sliced
- 2 tbsp cornflour (cornstarch)
- 400ml (1⅔ cups) beef or ham stock
- 80ml (⅓ cup) double (heavy) cream
- ½ tbsp chopped parsley
- ½ tsp Dijon mustard

SWEDISH MEATBALLS

Serves 3 ❊

Prep + Cook 25 mins

This was not surprisingly inspired by a certain Swedish chain of home stores that sells furniture I can afford, but food I can't eat - this dish included. So, of course, that was all the inspiration I needed to make my own version, which, much like flat-pack furniture, is easy to assemble, with simple instructions, and definitely won't last long in our house.

1 Preheat your oven to 200°C fan / 220°C / 425°F. Line a large baking sheet with foil and grease with a little oil.

2 Add all the ingredients for the meatballs to a large bowl and mix with a wooden spoon until well combined. Shape into 15 meatballs – I find the easiest way to do this is to use an ice-cream scoop, tightly compacting each into the scoop, then turning it out onto the prepared baking sheet. Place all the meatballs on the baking sheet and bake in the oven for 10-12 minutes, or until nicely browned. Optionally pop under the grill for 2 minutes for the ultimate crispy finish.

3 While the meatballs are cooking, make the sauce. Place a large pan over a medium heat and add the garlic-infused oil and butter. Once melted, add the mushrooms and fry until a little golden, then add the cornflour and stir until everything is evenly covered.

4 Next, add the stock, bring to the boil and simmer for 5 minutes until it thickens up a little. Stir in the cream, then add the parsley and mustard and mix in once again.

5 Simmer for another 5 minutes until the sauce has thickened to a gravy-like consistency. Place the meatballs in the sauce and stir gently to coat

6 Serve over mashed potatoes with a little cranberry sauce on the side.

use dairy-free cheese

 use 75g (3oz) oyster mushrooms (thinly sliced) instead of button mushrooms

 omit the bacon and use 50g (1¾oz) more button mushrooms instead; use extra-mature Cheddar instead of Parmesan

 follow the vegetarian advice but use dairy-free cheese

- 190g (6¾oz) gluten-free dried spaghetti
- 5 tbsp garlic-infused oil
- 2 slices of smoked bacon, finely chopped
- 100g (3½oz) button mushrooms, thinly sliced
- 3 tbsp finely grated Parmesan
- 1 tbsp dried or finely chopped fresh parsley
- ¼ tsp dried chilli flakes
- ½ tsp salt
- Pinch of black pepper
- 2 handfuls of rocket (arugula)

CRISPY BACON SPAGHETTI AGLIO E OLIO

Serves 2

Prep + Cook 15 mins

In case you couldn't read and/or pronounce the title, this is a classic Italian dish that translates as 'spaghetti with garlic and oil'. Traditionally, it's literally just spaghetti coated in garlic oil with a little seasoning. However, I like to make mine a little more of a full meal by adding crispy bacon and mushrooms. It's a super-speedy meal that has quickly become a weekly staple in our house.

1 Boil the spaghetti in salted water according to the packet instructions - gluten-free pasta can often clump together, but adding it straight to boiling water with 1 teaspoon of oil can massively help to prevent this.

2 Add 2 tablespoons of the garlic-infused oil to a large frying pan and place over a medium heat. Once hot, add the bacon and fry for 1–2 minutes, then add the mushrooms and fry until slightly golden.

3 Once cooked, drain the spaghetti and add straight to the pan. Stir briefly, then add the remaining garlic-infused oil, followed by the Parmesan, parsley, chilli flakes, salt and pepper. Stir in well until everything is evenly dispersed.

4 Serve immediately in bowls with a handful of rocket on top.

use a thick dairy-free yoghurt/cheese

 use lactose-free Greek yoghurt

 use lactose-free Greek yoghurt and ensure all toppings are FODMAP-friendly

 use veggie-friendly toppings and use extra-mature Cheddar instead of Parmesan

 use a thick dairy-free yoghurt/cheese and vegan-friendly toppings

---

For the dough

- 200g (1½ cups) gluten-free self-raising (self-rising) flour
- 205g (7½oz) Greek yoghurt (or any thick, natural yoghurt)
- Pinch of salt

For the sauce

- 140ml (⅔ cup) passata (sieved tomatoes)
- 1 tsp garlic-infused oil
- 2 tsp dried oregano
- 2 tbsp gluten-free BBQ sauce (optional: for a BBQ base)
- Salt and black pepper

For the toppings

- 6 slices of pepperoni
- 1 slice of honey-roast ham and 1 pineapple ring, diced
- 4–5 slices of Brie and 1 tbsp grated Parmesan
- 1 x 125g (4½oz) mozzarella ball
- Fresh basil leaves, to serve (optional)

ONE-SHEET PIZZA BUFFET

Makes 12 small or 6 large slices ❄
Prep + Cook 30 mins

Meet the ultimate people-pleasing pizza-in-a-hurry, with three different toppings on one super-thin and crispy base. There's no need to fry your base in a frying pan before finishing in the oven with this one – simply roll out, transfer to a baking sheet, top and shove straight into the oven. It's honestly the fastest way imaginable to make a pizza from scratch! I've provided our favourite toppings, but feel free to top with whatever you like.

1 Preheat your oven 240°C fan / 260°C / 500°F or as hot as it will go.

2 To make the dough, add the flour and yoghurt to a large mixing bowl and mix thoroughly using a spatula to ensure there are clumps. Use your hands to bring it together into a slightly sticky ball. Knead the dough briefly in the bowl until smooth, combined and no longer sticky. Dough still too sticky? Add a little more flour to the dough. Dough too dry? Add a little more yoghurt.

3 Transfer the dough to a large sheet of non-stick baking parchment. Lightly flour your rolling pin and roll out the dough to a large, even rectangle 1mm (⅟₃₂in) thick. Re-flour your rolling pin as necessary to stop it from sticking. Use the baking parchment to lift the rolled out dough onto a large baking tray. Form a crust around the dough by folding it over along the edges to create a 1cm (½in) ridge, then gently press it down.

4 Combine all the ingredients for the sauce in a small bowl, with salt and pepper to taste, then spread onto your base, right up to the outer ridge.

5 Top the left third of your pizza with pepperoni, the middle third with ham and pineapple and the final third with Brie and a sprinkling of Parmesan. Tear the mozzarella into small chunks and scatter evenly over the entire pizza.

6 Bake for 15 minutes, or until the cheese is nicely browned and golden. The oven is super-hot (like a pizza oven would be), so keep an eye on it for the last 5 minutes or so. Use the baking parchment to lift the pizza onto a flat surface and cut into 12 small or 6 large slices. Finish with some fresh basil leaves, if you like, and serve immediately.

TIP If using a different type of yoghurt that isn't quite as thick, simply add a little more flour to compensate.

use dairy-free butter, milk, cheese and a dairy-free natural yoghurt instead of crème fraîche

 use lactose-free milk and lactose-free yoghurt instead of crème fraîche

 use lactose-free milk and lactose-free yoghurt instead of crème fraîche

---

- 1 fillet each of salmon, cod and smoked haddock, chopped
- 185g (6½oz) crème fraîche
- 1 tbsp finely chopped chives
- 60g (2oz) frozen peas
- 100g (3½oz) raw, shelled prawns (shrimp), deveined
- 50g (1¾oz) smoked salmon
- Salt and black pepper

For the topping

- 750g–1kg (1lb 10oz–2lb 4oz) potatoes, peeled and chopped into chunks
- 50g (3½ tbsp) butter
- Splash of milk
- 1 tsp wholegrain mustard
- 1 tbsp finely chopped chives
- 50g (1¾oz) Cheddar, grated

QUICK FISH PIE

Serves 4-6 ❄

Prep + Cook 30 mins

In ordinary circumstances, whipping up a fish pie in 30 minutes is nigh on impossible. However, using crème fraîche instead of creating a white sauce, it suddenly becomes mission possible! With lots of tender, moist fish, prawns and flecks of smoked salmon hiding underneath a bed of creamy, mustard mash, this is definitely 30 minutes well spent.

1 Preheat your oven to 220°C fan / 240°C / 465°F.

2 Cook the potatoes in a large saucepan of boiling water for 10-12 minutes until tender, then drain and mash with the butter, milk, mustard, chives, and salt and pepper to taste.

3 Meanwhile, in a separate pan of simmering water, poach your chopped salmon, cod and smoked haddock for about 5 minutes. Drain, return to the pan and carefully stir in the crème fraîche, chives, frozen peas and prawns.

4 Spoon the fish mixture into an ovenproof dish, about 18 x 28cm (7 x 11in). Pull the smoked salmon into pieces and dot it on top, then cover with the mashed potatoes and sprinkle with grated cheese.

5 Bake in the oven for 10-12 minutes until the top is starting to turn golden.

TIP For an even more golden top, leave in the oven for an extra 5 minutes or pop under the grill for the final couple of minutes to brown.

use a low FODMAP stock cube

 use a gluten-free veggie/vegan stock cube

 follow the vegetarian advice above

- 300ml (1½ cups) boiling water
- 2 dried vermicelli rice noodle nests (100g/3½oz in total)
- 1 gluten-free chicken stock cube

For plain chicken noodles

- Pinch of black pepper
- 1 tsp dried parsley
- Pinch of ground turmeric
- 1 tsp garlic-infused oil

For chow-mein-style noodles

- 1 tsp gluten-free soy sauce
- ¼ tsp ground ginger
- Pinch of black pepper
- ¼ tsp five spice
- 1 tsp garlic-infused oil

For curry noodles

- ½ tsp gluten-free soy sauce
- ½ tsp mild curry powder
- Pinch of ground turmeric
- Pinch of five spice
- 1 tsp dried parsley
- Pinch of dried chilli flakes
- 1 tsp garlic-infused oil

SUPER-INSTANT NOODLES

Serves 2

Prep + Cook 5 mins

Here's a strange thing to admit: I've been extensively studying the ingredients lists on the backs of packet instant noodles that I haven't eaten in over a decade. But it's all in the name of making my own gluten-free versions! And I can honestly say to you that it was worth it! Here are three variations to get you started, but feel free to use this recipe to create your own flavours too.

1 Pour the boiling water into a large saucepan, then add the noodles, crumble in the stock cube, place over a medium heat and bring to the boil.

2 Once boiling, give the noodles a good stir so they're not clumped up, then add the ingredients for the flavouring of your choice. Reduce the heat to low and simmer for about 4 minutes, or until all the liquid has evaporated.

3 Turn off the heat and allow to stand for 1 minute. This will allow the noodles to magically dry out a little and be perfect to eat – straight from the pan if you must!

TIP There's no need for any salt here! Stock cubes usually have more than enough. If your stock cubes are particularly salty, consider using ¾ of a stock cube instead of a whole one.

- 3 tbsp garlic-infused oil
- 3 large boneless, skinless chicken thighs (about 400g/14oz in total), sliced into thin strips
- 1 green (bell) pepper, sliced into strips
- 1 yellow (bell) pepper, sliced into strips
- ½ red onion, cut into chunks, or ½ medium courgette (zucchini), cut into batons 1cm (½in) wide and 5cm (2in) long
- 2 handfuls of gluten-free tortilla chips, roughly crushed with your hands
- 3 tbsp gluten-free BBQ sauce

For the spice blend
- ½ tsp cayenne pepper
- 1 tsp ground cumin
- 2 tsp dried oregano
- 1 tbsp smoked paprika
- 1 tsp salt

To serve
- 4-6 gluten-free tortilla wraps, warmed
- 1 small avocado, peeled, pitted and smashed
- 8 tbsp salsa

Pictured on page 108

ONE-SHEET BBQ CHICKEN CRUNCH FAJITAS

Serves 2–3
Prep + Cook 25 mins

This recipe is so incredibly easy that, when I make it, I honestly feel like I'm not even cooking at all! Get those gluten-free wraps ready for succulent, smoky BBQ chicken, perfectly charred peppers, finished with a deeply satisfying crunch from the crushed, toasted tortilla chips. You'd never guess it was made by throwing it all onto one tray and shoving it in the oven!

1 Preheat your oven to 210°C fan / 230°C / 450°F and lightly grease a large baking tray with 1 tablespoon of the garlic-infused oil.

2 In a small bowl, mix together the ingredients for the spice blend.

3 Add the chicken, peppers and onion or courgette to the oiled baking tray and spread out in an even layer. Drizzle over the remaining garlic-infused oil and sprinkle over the spice blend. Turn everything over a few times so it is evenly coated.

4 Bake in the oven for 13-15 minutes, then remove and sprinkle the crushed tortilla chips over the veg and chicken. Return to the oven for 7-8 minutes until the chicken is cooked and the peppers are completely softened, then remove from the oven and dollop the BBQ sauce around the tray.

5 Mix everything up so that it's all evenly coated in the BBQ sauce, and serve up immediately with warm gluten-free tortilla wraps, smashed avocado and salsa.

SPEEDY SIDES

I was going to start this by writing something like 'what's Batman without Robin?' but as many successful movies without his sidekick have proved, Robin might have actually been holding him back...

But superheroes and awkward chapter intros aside, I think we can all agree that a selection of good sides can make a meal great, right? So a better analogy might be: what's a curry without a naan? What's a Chinese takeaway without proper fried rice?

But when cooking at home, if a side involves more time, effort and washing up than the main dish, suddenly all my sides mysteriously cease to exist. And unlike Batman without Robin, that's definitely not a good thing!

That's why I've created an entire chapter of sides that are super-quick and easy to rustle up in 30 minutes or less. So bring on the speedy sides!

use grated dairy-free cheese, pesto, cream cheese and a thick dairy-free yoghurt

 use lactose-free Greek yoghurt and cream cheese

 use lactose-free Greek yoghurt and cream cheese, and use a low FODMAP pesto

 use extra-mature Cheddar instead of Parmesan and ensure the pesto is veggie-friendly

 use grated dairy-free cheese, pesto, cream cheese and a thick dairy-free yoghurt

---

- 260g (2 cups) gluten-free self-raising (self-rising) flour
- 260g (1¼ cups) Greek yoghurt (or any thick, natural yoghurt)
- 3 tbsp cream cheese
- Pinch of salt
- 2 tbsp garlic-infused oil, plus 2 tbsp for the tops
- 30g (1oz) pesto
- 1 x 125g mozzarella ball, cut into chunks 2cm (¾in) long, 1cm (½in) wide
- 4 tbsp grated Parmesan
- 1 tbsp finely chopped parsley, to finish

TRIPLE CHEESE PESTO DOUGH BALLS

Makes 12 ❄

Prep + Cook 30 mins

There are a million things you can make with a combo of self-raising flour and Greek yoghurt, so here's one of them. Each dough ball has cream cheese in the dough, is stuffed with mozzarella and pesto, then brushed with garlic oil and topped with Parmesan.

1 Preheat your oven to 200°C fan / 220°C / 425°F.

2 Put the flour and yoghurt (give it a good stir before using) into a large mixing bowl. Mix together using a spatula and, as it starts to come together, add the cream cheese, salt and garlic-infused oil and mix in until combined. Once it forms a smooth dough, use your hands to bring it together into a slightly sticky ball.

3 Pull off a portion of the dough and roll it into a golf-ball-sized ball (mine weighed 50g/1¾oz). Flatten in your hands before adding around a ¼ teaspoon pesto and a chunk of mozzarella to the middle. Fold shut like a taco and mould back into a ball, then roll in your hands to smooth the exterior. Repeat with the remaining dough and fillings.

4 Place on a large baking sheet, spacing them around 2.5cm (1in) apart, and brush each ball with garlic-infused oil. Sprinkle over the Parmesan and bake in the oven for 15 minutes, or until the tops are a little golden brown. Sprinkle with fresh parsley to finish.

- Vegetable oil, for frying
- 3 leaves of fresh greens or 5 big Savoy cabbage leaves
- 1 tsp light brown sugar
- ½ tsp five spice
- ¼ tsp salt

Pictured on page 69

CRISPY SEAWEED

Serves 2–3

Prep + Cook 15 mins

I hate to break it to you, but crispy seaweed that you'd get from your local Chinese takeaway isn't actually made from seaweed! But fortunately, it's incredibly easy to replicate at home with no worry of cross-contamination from fryers.

1 Pour vegetable oil into a large, deep saucepan to around a 1cm (½in) depth. Place over a medium heat until the oil reaches 160°C (320°F). If you don't have a digital food thermometer, use the wooden spoon handle test (page 16).

2 Prepare your greens or cabbage leaves by removing the stalks on each leaf using a sharp knife. Next, pile the leaves on top of each over, fold in half and then roll up tightly. Chop the leaves into thin strips about a 5mm (¼in) wide. Mix the sugar, five spice and salt together in a small dish.

3 Once your oil has reached the desired temperature, lower the shredded greens or cabbage into the oil and fry for 3 minutes, or until crispy. It will initially bubble up a lot, which is why using a deep pan is really important! Transfer to a plate lined with kitchen paper and allow to drain.

4 Once drained, transfer the fried cabbage to a serving dish and sprinkle on the five spice mixture. Toss briefly until well coated, then serve immediately.

To cook in an air fryer

Preheat the air fryer to 200°C (400°F). Prepare the fresh greens or savoy cabbage and five spice mixture as described in step 2. Place the chopped greens into a large mixing bowl and generously spray with vegetable oil. Place into the air fryer for 6–8 minutes until crisp. Transfer to a serving dish and sprinkle on the five spice mixture. Toss briefly until well coated, then serve immediately.

TIP Only the outer leaves are fit for frying in this recipe, so, basically, the greener the better. The inner leaves are whiter and will turn browner when cooked (but still taste fine) but the very inside leaves contain too much moisture to turn crisp. Not all types of cabbage or fresh greens will turn crisp when fried - some will just turn limp and soggy! So make sure it's Savoy cabbage, or kale as a back-up option; though in my opinion, Savoy cabbage tastes and fries better!

crumble in 125g (4½oz) extra-firm tofu (instead of the eggs) with a pinch of turmeric

---

- 2 x 250g (9oz) microwaveable packets of rice or 500g (1lb 2oz) cooked rice, ideally chilled
- 2 tbsp garlic-infused oil
- 2 medium eggs
- 1 tsp minced ginger
- 4 tbsp sesame oil
- 4 tbsp gluten-free soy sauce
- 50g (1¾oz) frozen peas
- 100g (3½oz) fresh pineapple chunks
- Handful of cashew nuts
- ¼ tsp dried chilli flakes (optional)

Pictured on page 68

PINEAPPLE AND CASHEW NUT FRIED RICE

Serves 3-4

Prep + Cook 15 mins

Meet the Chinese fakeaway side that's so good I'd happily just eat it on its own! It's mildly spicy, savoury and sweet, thanks to the pineapple, with chunks of egg, cashew nuts and boatloads of flavour.

1 Cook your rice according to the packet instructions. Optionally pop the rice into an airtight container once completely cooled and chill in the fridge overnight, if you have time.

2 Add the garlic-infused oil to a wok and place over a medium-high heat. Once hot, crack in the eggs, break the yolks and allow to sit for around 1 minute. Break up the egg into chunks, before adding your cooked rice, stirring to break it up. Once it's a little more separated, add the minced ginger and sesame oil, then stir well to coat the rice and egg.

3 Add the soy sauce and stir once again so the rice is nicely coated and doesn't look so white.

4 Add the frozen peas, pineapple, cashew nuts and chilli flakes, if using, and stir once more. Stir-fry for 5 minutes, or until the rice starts to look a little drier and crisper in places, and is piping hot. If you didn't have time to allow your rice to fully cool or chill in the fridge, you'll likely need to fry for a little longer to reach that point. Serve immediately.

use dairy-free milk and a good dairy-free cheese that melts well

 use lactose-free milk

 use dairy-free milk and a good dairy-free cheese that melts well

---

- 300g (10½oz) cauliflower florets (about 1 small cauliflower), cut into bite-sized chunks
- 200g (7oz) broccoli florets (about 1 small head of broccoli), cut into bite-sized chunks
- 2-3 tbsp gluten-free breadcrumbs

For the cheese sauce
- 50g (3½ tbsp) butter
- 60g (½ cup) gluten-free plain (all-purpose) flour
- 750ml (3 cups) milk
- 125g (4½oz) extra-mature Cheddar, grated
- 2 tsp wholegrain mustard (optional)
- Salt and black pepper

MUM'S BROCCOLI AND CAULIFLOWER CHEESE

Serves 4-6 ❄

Prep 15 mins **+ Cook** 15 mins

I took my mum's classic broccoli and cauliflower cheese recipe and sped it up a little; I don't think she'd notice the difference! I added a little more flour to the white sauce so it comes together more quickly and I even blast my veg in the microwave, which saves a precious few minutes. Of course, you can always boil your veg too, but it'll take you over the 30-minute mark for sure.

1 Preheat your oven to 200°C fan / 220°C / 425°F.

To prepare the veg on the hob

Place the cauliflower in a large saucepan, fill just under halfway with boiling water, then bring to the boil over a medium heat. Once boiling, cook for 5 minutes, then add the broccoli and cook for a further 3 minutes. Drain and set aside.

To prepare the veg in the microwave (slightly quicker)

Place the cauliflower and broccoli in a medium, heatproof bowl, add 5 tablespoons of water and cover with a large dinner plate. Microwave on full power (900W) for 5 minutes, then allow to steam without removing the plate on top for 2-3 minutes more. Drain any remaining water and set aside.

2 While the veg is cooking, make the sauce. Add the butter, flour and milk to a large saucepan and mix in thoroughly so that all the flour is no longer visible and lumpy. Place over a medium heat until the butter has melted, then turn the heat down to low. At this point, you need to stir constantly it until it has transformed into a lovely, thick sauce, around 3-5 minutes. Stir in the grated cheese and mustard, if using, then season with salt and pepper to taste.

3 Grab a medium roasting dish (mine is a 18 x 28cm/7 x 11in rectangular dish) and add the broccoli and cauliflower. Pour over the sauce and scatter the breadcrumbs on top, right up to the edges.

4 Place the dish on a baking tray and bake for 12-15 minutes, or until the breadcrumbs are wonderfully golden and any exposed cheese sauce is nicely browned.

- 500g (1lb 2oz) frozen oven chips (ensure gluten-free)
- 1 tbsp garlic-infused oil

For the spice blend
- ½ tsp five spice
- ½ tsp ground ginger
- ½ tsp black pepper
- ½ tsp dried chilli flakes
- ½ tsp salt

CHINESE TAKE-OUT-STYLE SALT AND PEPPER CHIPS

Serves 3–4

Prep + Cook 20 mins

This salt and pepper spice blend instantly transforms any frozen chips into a takeaway-worthy side. They're spicy, with a wonderful blend of aromatic ginger and spice that belong on any good fakeaway plate.

1 Cook the frozen oven chips according to the packet instructions.

2 In a small bowl, mix the spice blend ingredients together.

3 Drizzle the cooked chips with the garlic-infused oil and mix until evenly and lightly coated.

4 Sprinkle half the spice blend over the chips, ensuring you don't chuck loads on at once, or they will be very unevenly coated!

5 Toss all the chips once again until the seasoning is evenly dispersed, then repeat with the rest of the seasoning. If some get a little too much in one place, simply keep mixing until they are all a little more consistently coated.

AIR FRYER CHIPS

Serves 2-3 ❄

Prep + Cook 15 mins

I'm pretty sure that whenever anyone gets an air fryer, the first thing they make are chips. So here's a recipe to get you started that will keep you happily air frying for months and years to come, if you're anything like I am. Being able to cook potato from raw this fast just isn't possible in the oven, so take advantage of it!

1 Add all the ingredients to a medium bowl and mix until well coated.

2 Preheat the air fryer by setting it to 200°C (400°F) or as high as it will go if it doesn't reach this temperature, and set the timer to 18 minutes.

3 Once hot, add the chips to the air fryer basket and close the lid.

4 After 10 minutes, turn them over and continue to cook for the remaining time. A few minutes before they finish, it's always good to check on the chips to ensure they're not browning too much. Of course, if they're not particularly golden yet, you can always add an extra 3-5 minutes too.

- 2 medium-large potatoes, cut into chips 1cm (½in) thick
- 1-2 tbsp oil or garlic-infused oil
- 1 tsp salt
- ½ tsp black pepper
- 1 tbsp dried rosemary (optional)

Pictured on page 112

- 1 small onion (about 225g/8oz)
- Vegetable oil, for frying
- 4 tbsp gluten-free plain (all-purpose) flour

For the batter
- 125g (1 cup minus 1 tsp) gluten-free plain (all-purpose) flour
- ½ tsp gluten-free baking powder
- 1 tsp salt
- 150ml (⅝ cup) gluten-free beer or carbonated water

BEER-BATTERED ONION RINGS

Serves 4 ❄

Prep + Cook 25 mins

As you might know, I sadly struggle to tolerate onion, so this is most definitely a recipe created purely for you lot! Using a slightly thickened version of my beer batter, I created a super-simple recipe that results in golden, crispy battered onion rings every time.

1 Slice the onion (without peeling) into rings about 1cm (½in) wide. Remove the outer skin and separate into as many rings as possible.

2 Pour enough oil into a large, heavy-based wok or frying pan until a third full. Place over a medium heat for 8–10 minutes, or until it reaches 170°C (340°F). If you don't have a digital food thermometer, use the wooden spoon handle test (page 16). Line a large plate with kitchen paper, ready for later.

3 While the oil is heating, combine all the dry ingredients for the batter in a large mixing bowl. Give it a whisk so it's all nicely mixed. Don't add the beer or carbonated water until your oil is ready or it'll lose its fizz.

4 Grab a large plate and spread the 4 tablespoons of flour on it. Place the sliced onion rings on the plate and roll around until lightly coated. Don't skip this step or the batter won't stick!

5 Add the beer or carbonated water to the dry batter ingredients and whisk until consistent.

6 Dredge the floured rings in the batter mixture, then carefully lower 4–5 into the hot oil. Cook for 4 minutes until the batter is golden and crispy, turning halfway. Using carbonated water means it'll be a little lighter in colour, so bear that in mind. Once cooked, remove from the oil using a slotted spoon, and place on a plate lined with kitchen paper to drain. Repeat with the remaining onion rings.

use a thick dairy-free yoghurt

 use lactose-free Greek yoghurt

 use lactose-free Greek yoghurt

 use a thick dairy-free yoghurt

- 250g (generous 1¾ cups) gluten-free self-raising (self-rising) flour, plus extra for dusting
- 260g (1¼ cups) Greek yoghurt (or any thick, natural yoghurt)
- 2 tsp nigella seeds
- Pinch of salt

Pictured on page 96

 use a dairy-free 'buttery' margarine

 ensure your bread is low FODMAP and use garlic-infused oil instead of minced garlic paste

 use a dairy-free 'buttery' margarine

- 4 gluten-free white ciabatta rolls
- Flaky salt

For the topping
- ½ tbsp dried parsley
- 2 tbsp garlic-infused oil or 2 tsp minced garlic paste
- 2 tbsp very soft butter

SPEEDY NAAN

Makes 4 ❄

Prep + Cook 20 mins

With no yeast and no proving, these are the fastest naan to make in all the land! Plus they only call for three ingredients and a pinch of salt, so you can whip these up while your curry is simmering.

1 Mix all the ingredients together in a large mixing bowl, then use your hands to bring it together into a slightly sticky ball. On a well-floured surface, knead the dough briefly until smooth, combined and no longer sticky. Divide the dough into 4 equal pieces and use a lightly floured rolling pin to roll out each dough portion to a 3mm (⅛in) thickness, aiming for an oval shape.

2 Place a large frying pan over a high heat. Once very hot, carefully transfer a naan bread to the dry frying pan, using a cake lifter or a pizza peel. Cook for 2 minutes, or until nicely browned underneath, then flip and cook for 1 minute. After flipping, press down firmly on the naan using a spatula – this encourages the naan to puff up a little. Repeat with the remaining dough.

CHEAT'S GARLIC BREAD

Makes 8 mini garlic breads ❄

Prep + Cook 20 mins

Fortunately for us, I've found that there's always been a healthy supply of gluten-free bread in supermarket 'free from'/gluten-free aisles. So why not take advantage of that? You can easily turn a modest gluten-free ciabatta roll into glorious garlic bread with next to no effort, in no time!

1 Preheat your oven to 200°C fan / 220°C / 425°F. Cut the ciabatta rolls in half and place cut-side up on a large baking sheet.

2 In a small bowl, mix the ingredients for the topping together until smooth. Spread the mixture over the ciabatta rolls, right up to the edges. Place into the oven for 8–10 minutes until golden and crisp, then top each with a pinch of flaky salt to serve.

use dairy-free milk

 use lactose-free milk

 use lactose-free milk

- 2 tbsp vegetable oil
- 100g (1 cup minus 1½ tbsp) cornflour (cornstarch)
- 3 medium eggs
- 150ml (⅝ cup) milk

3-INGREDIENT XL YORKSHIRE PUDDINGS

Makes two 20cm (8in) Yorkshire puddings ❄
Prep 5 mins **+ Cook** 20 mins

Ever since Nigella Lawson gave her seal of approval to my gluten-free Yorkshire puddings, I haven't been able to shut up about it. But what most people don't realize is that you can use my original recipe to create two large Yorkshire puddings that are fit for serving a roast dinner inside of, or slicing up into individual portions. These never fail to elicit 'oohs' and 'ahhs' from your guests as they puff up to be so huge in the oven.

1 Preheat your oven to 200°C fan / 220°C / 425°F. Grab two 20cm (8in) cake tins (pans) and add 1 tablespoon of oil to each. Place in the oven to heat for 10–12 minutes.

2 Put the cornflour and eggs into a large mixing bowl. Whisk together until smooth, then add half the milk and whisk until free of lumps. Add the other half of the milk and whisk in.

3 Remove the cake tins from the oven and quickly pour half of the batter into each one – it should sizzle a little. Immediately return to the oven and cook for 20 minutes until browned, crispy and miraculously risen. Please never open the oven during cooking to check on it as this will cause it to instantly deflate!

4 Either cut each Yorkshire pudding in two and serve alongside a roast dinner, or plate up and fill with a serving of one tray chicken roast dinner (page 103) or beef or chicken stew (page 98).

PARTY FOOD

If you're gluten-free, I'm sure you can already guess why this chapter exists. But here's the answer anyway: being gluten-free around any sort of buffet scenario is an absolute nightmare!

Not only do you have no idea what's actually gluten-free (if anything) but even if there are gluten-free options, they're often way too close to all the gluten-containing food for comfort.

So what's the solution? Host your own parties and family gatherings and make the entire buffet gluten-free! But wait; won't everyone turn their noses up if everything is gluten-free?

Well, in my experience, if you have the right recipes then nobody will even notice that the entire spread is gluten-free. And no, that doesn't mean that everything has to be some form of fruit salad.

Here's a chapter of all my gluten-free party food favourites that'll please coeliacs and muggles alike. If you are intending to create multiple recipes from this chapter for your 100% gluten-free buffet, you'll be pleased to know that anything that needs to go in the oven can all go in 200°C fan / 220°C / 425°F. That way, you can prepare them ahead of time and shove them in all at once.

Just making one recipe as a side or as a supplement to store-bought party food? Not surprisingly, all of these recipes can be made in <u>30 minutes or less</u>, so you can concentrate on the important stuff: your guests!

- Vegetable oil, for greasing
- 280g (10oz) store-bought gluten-free puff pastry (see TIP if using homemade)
- 1 egg, beaten
- 3 tbsp nigella seeds
- Mango chutney, to serve

For the filling

- 300g (10½oz) pork mince (ground pork) or gluten-free sausage meat
- 2 tsp garlic-infused oil
- 1½ tbsp cornflour (cornstarch)
- 1 tsp minced ginger paste
- ½ tsp dried chilli flakes
- Pinch each of salt and black pepper
- 1½ tsp mild curry powder
- 2 tsp finely chopped fresh coriander (cilantro)

CURRIED SAUSAGE ROLLS + MANGO CHUTNEY

Makes 16 ❀

Prep + Cook 30 mins

A simple spice blend takes these to an entirely different planet in terms of flavour, and when paired with mango chutney, it's a world I wouldn't mind visiting as often as possible.

1 Preheat your oven to 200°C fan / 220°C / 425°F. Lightly grease a large baking sheet and line with non-stick baking parchment.

2 Put the filling ingredients into a large bowl and give it all a good mix until evenly combined.

3 Unroll the pastry on a work surface with a long side closest to you. Use a pizza cutter (I also use a long ruler to ensure I'm cutting straight) to cut in half horizontally, so you have 2 equal strips.

4 Divide the filling between each pastry strip in a long line, slightly below the middle of each strip. Brush the smaller side of the exposed pastry with beaten egg. Fold the larger side of the pastry over the filling. Using your fingers, gently form the pastry around the filling to compact it and remove any gaps. Crimp the pastry all along the seam using a fork to securely seal it shut. Use a large, sharp knife to cut into 4cm (1½in) mini sausage rolls, then transfer to the prepared baking sheet. Brush each sausage roll with beaten egg, then sprinkle over the nigella seeds.

5 Bake in the oven for 10 minutes, or until the pastry is golden, then cover loosely with foil and cook for a further 7–10 minutes. Remove from the oven and place on a wire rack to cool for 10 minutes. Serve with mango chutney as a dip and enjoy hot, warm or cold.

To cook in an air fryer

Preheat the air fryer to 200°C (400°F) and spray a little oil into the tray. Place as many sausage rolls in the air fryer basket as will fit without touching. Cook for 5 minutes, then cover with foil and cook for a further 5–8 minutes.

TIP If using homemade gluten-free rough puff pastry (see the recipe in my first or second books), simply roll out to a 20 x 30cm (8 x 12in) rectangle around 3mm (⅛in) thick, and proceed as directed above.

use dairy-free cheese

 LL

 use low FODMAP pepperoni

 omit the pepperoni

 use dairy-free cheese, omit the pepperoni and use vegan mayo for the dip

---

- Vegetable oil, for greasing
- 280g (10oz) store-bought gluten-free puff pastry (see TIP if using homemade)
- 50g (1¾oz) grated mozzarella
- 12 slices of pepperoni

For the pizza sauce

- 80ml (⅓ cup) passata (sieved tomatoes)
- 1 tsp garlic-infused oil
- 1 tsp dried oregano, mixed herbs or Italian seasoning
- Pinch each of salt and black pepper

For the garlic and herb dip (optional)

- 100ml (scant ½ cup) mayonnaise
- 1½ tsp garlic-infused oil
- 1½ tsp dried oregano, mixed herbs or Italian seasoning

Pictured on page 151

PEPPERONI PIZZA PUFFS

Makes 12

Prep + Cook 20 mins

Nothing says party like pizza! And puff pastry pizza might even be my new favourite kind. You can make this recipe quicker by using a jar of pizza sauce too, but I'll leave that decision down to you.

1 Preheat your oven to 200°C fan / 220°C / 425°F. Lightly grease two baking sheets.

2 In a small bowl, combine all the ingredients for the pizza sauce. Set aside.

3 Unroll the pastry on a work surface with a long side closest to you. Use a pizza cutter (I also use a long ruler to ensure I'm cutting straight) to cut horizontally, dividing the pastry into 3 equal strips. Then cut vertically 4 times, to create 12 individual 4cm (1½in) pastry squares.

4 Spread a generous teaspoon of pizza sauce onto each square, using the back of the spoon to spread the sauce right up to the edges. Top with grated mozzarella and a slice of pepperoni. Use a palette knife to transfer the pizza puffs to the baking sheets, spacing them apart a little.

5 Bake in the oven for 6 minutes until the cheese is lovely and golden, then cover loosely with foil and cook for a further 4 minutes. Meanwhile, mix up the ingredients for the dip, if serving, in a small dish.

6 Serve the squares hot from the oven alongside the dip, or by themselves.

To cook in an air fryer

Preheat the air fryer to 200°C (400°F) and spray a little oil into the tray. Follow the steps above to create the pizza puffs and place as many into the air fryer basket as will fit without touching. Cook for 3–4 minutes before covering loosely with an appropriately sized piece of foil, then cook for a further 2–3 minutes, or until the cheese is nicely browned.

TIP If using homemade gluten-free rough puff pastry (see the recipe in my first or second books), simply roll out to a 20 x 30cm (8 x 12in) rectangle around 3mm (⅛in) thick, and proceed as directed above.

use 100ml (scant ½ cup) dairy-free milk mixed with 1 tsp lemon juice instead of the eggs; allow to rest for 10 minutes then continue with the recipe as directed

---

- Garlic-infused oil, for greasing and drizzling/spraying
- 3 tbsp cornflour (cornstarch)
- 2 medium eggs
- 200–250g (7–9oz) button mushrooms

For the breadcrumb coating
- 70g (2½oz) gluten-free breadcrumbs
- 1 tsp dried oregano
- ¼ tsp dried chilli flakes
- 1 tsp smoked paprika
- 1 tsp salt
- ¼ tsp white or black pepper

Pictured on page 150

CRISPY SOUTHERN-FRIED MUSHROOMS

Makes about 25 ✽
Prep + Cook 15 mins

Is it even a party if at least 50% of the food isn't covered in breadcrumbs? While I'm not a huge mushroom fan unless they're coated in a thick sauce, these are a welcome exception. They're super-juicy and coated in the breadcrumb and spice mix I'd usually use to create southern-fried chicken – it's a little spicy, smoky, crunchy and oh-so-good.

1 Preheat your oven to 200°C fan / 220°C / 425°F. Lightly oil a baking sheet and line with non-stick baking parchment.

2 Spread the cornflour onto a large plate. Crack the eggs into a medium bowl and lightly beat with a fork. Put the coating ingredients into another bowl and stir to combine.

3 Place the mushrooms on the cornflour plate and roll around until evenly coated. Transfer half the mushrooms to the egg bowl and mix around until well coated, then transfer them to the breadcrumb bowl and mix around until completely coated on all sides. If you have any dry white patches, simply dip those parts back into the egg and return to the breadcrumb bowl.

4 Transfer to the prepared baking sheet, drizzle with a little garlic-infused oil and repeat until all the mushrooms are coated.

5 Bake in the oven for 15 minutes, flipping them over halfway, until the breadcrumbs are golden.

To cook in an air fryer

Preheat the air fryer to 200°C (400°F) and spray a little oil into the tray. Place as many coated mushrooms in the air fryer basket as will fit without touching, then generously spray with oil. Cook for 10 minutes, or until the breadcrumbs are golden and crispy.

use dairy-free cheese

 use extra Cheddar instead of Parmesan

 use dairy-free cheese

- Vegetable oil, for greasing
- 40g (1½oz) extra-mature Cheddar, finely grated
- 40g (1½oz) Red Leicester cheese, finely grated
- 4 tbsp finely grated Parmesan
- 280g (10oz) store-bought gluten-free puff pastry (see TIP if using homemade)
- Gluten-free plain (all-purpose) flour, for dusting

Pictured on page 151

5-INGREDIENT TRIPLE CHEESE STRAWS

Serves 3–4

Prep + Cook 20 mins

I don't think I've met a person who doesn't love a good cheese straw, but I have met loads of people who can't eat them! So here's an easy-peasy-cheesy gluten-free version that simply involves a little grated cheese and a bit of folding and rolling.

1 Preheat your oven to 200°C fan / 220°C / 425°F. Lightly grease two baking sheets. Mix the grated cheeses together in a medium bowl.

2 Unroll the pastry on a work surface and set aside. Lay flat the parchment paper that the pastry was rolled in. Sprinkle the paper with a quarter of the grated cheese so it's lightly covered, then place the pastry sheet on top. With a long side of the pastry closest to you, sprinkle with another quarter of the grated cheese, then fold the pastry over in half and shut it like a book.

3 Next, rotate the pastry 90 degrees so a long side is closest to you again and sprinkle the rest of the cheese onto the exposed paper underneath the pastry, reserving a small amount for the top. Sprinkle the remaining cheese on top of the pastry.

4 Using a lightly floured rolling pin, roll the pastry sheet out to a 1mm (⅟₃₂in) thickness, aiming for a large rectangle.

5 With a long side of the pastry closest to you, cut the pastry sheet into 2cm (¾in) strips. Grab a strip and, holding each end in either hand, twist twice and place on a baking sheet. Repeat until all your strips are twisted.

6 Bake in the oven for 10 minutes, then cover loosely with foil and cook for a further 3 minutes.

To cook in an air fryer

Preheat the air fryer to 200°C (400°F) and spray a little oil into the tray. Place as many strips in the air fryer basket as will fit without touching. Cook for 4 minutes before covering loosely with an appropriately sized piece of foil, then cook for a further 4–5 minutes.

TIP If using homemade gluten-free rough puff pastry (see the recipe in my first or second books), simply roll out to a 20 x 30cm (8 x 12in) rectangle around 3mm (⅛in) thick, and proceed as directed above.

- Vegetable oil, for frying
- 50g (½ cup minus 1 tbsp) cornflour (cornstarch)
- 330g (11½oz) large raw prawns (shrimp), shelled and deveined

For the batter

- 70g (½ cup plus ½ tbsp) gluten-free plain (all-purpose) flour
- 4 tbsp cornflour (cornstarch)
- 1 tsp gluten-free baking powder
- Pinch each of salt and black or white pepper
- 140ml (½ cup plus 1½ tbsp) gluten-free beer or carbonated water

Pictured on page 150

BEER-BATTERED TEMPURA PRAWNS

Serves 4 ❄

Prep + Cook 20 mins

There's something about tempura prawns (shrimp) that has become synonymous with party food and I'm not quite sure when it happened; but I'm very glad it did! These prawns are coated in a light tempura batter, but I switched up the carbonated water for gluten-free beer as a little twist. Of course, feel free to use either depending on your dietary requirements, but using beer gives them a more golden colour.

1 Pour vegetable oil into a large, heavy-based wok until around a third full. Place over a medium heat until it reaches 170°C (340°F). If you don't have a digital food thermometer, use the wooden spoon handle test (page 16). Line a large plate with kitchen paper, ready for later.

2 While the oil is heating, spread the cornflour onto a large plate. In a large mixing bowl, combine all the dry batter ingredients together and mix until consistent. Pour in the beer or carbonated water and whisk until the batter is smooth and lump-free.

3 Take half the prawns and roll them around on the cornflour plate until completely covered, then transfer them to the batter bowl and gently mix until well coated.

4 Once the oil is hot enough, carefully lower the coated prawns into the oil one at a time - they should sizzle nicely and sink to the bottom, then float to the top after 5 seconds or so. Make sure they're not touching each other in the wok, or they will stick together.

5 Cook for about 2 minutes, or until the batter goes from being pale to more golden. Once cooked, remove from the oil with a slotted spoon and transfer to the plate lined with kitchen paper. Repeat the coating and frying process using the rest of the prawns.

6 Serve up with your favourite gluten-free sweet chilli dipping sauce.

TIP If you don't use the wet batter straight away, ensure you give it a mix before using or the cornflour will sink to the bottom.

use dairy-free milk and ensure all toppings are dairy-free

 use lactose-free milk and ensure all toppings are lactose-free

 use lactose-free milk and ensure all toppings are FODMAP-friendly

 use veggie-friendly toppings

 use dairy-free milk, use a flax egg instead of the egg (see TIP on page 168), and use vegan-friendly toppings

---

- 150g (1 cup plus 2 tbsp) gluten-free self-raising (self-rising) flour
- ½ tsp salt
- 250ml (1 cup) milk
- 1 medium egg
- Vegetable oil, for frying

For the topping suggestions

- Smoked salmon, cream cheese and finely chopped chives
- Baked beans with sausages (canned), grated Cheddar and finely chopped chives
- Roasted five spice duck, gluten-free hoisin sauce and and cucumber and spring onion (scallion) strips
- Dollops of sour cream and finely chopped chives
- Dollops of mashed avocado, topped with a little salsa, grated cheese and a fresh coriander (cilantro) leaf

EASY-PEASY BLINIS

Makes 12–16 ❄

Prep + Cook 20 mins

Making your own blinis is no harder than making lots of mini pancakes, which you can then top with whatever you like. I always think of posh parties when I think of blinis for some reason, but in reality, they can be whatever you want them to be! I've provided a few topping suggestions, but feel free to use your own too.

1 In a large mixing bowl, combine the flour and the salt. In a jug (pitcher), beat together the milk and egg until smooth.

2 Create a well in the flour and pour in the wet mixture, while whisking thoroughly. After 30 seconds of whisking, it should be smooth, like a thin cream but not runny like water. Allow the batter to rest for 5 minutes.

3 Place a large frying pan over a low to medium heat. Add 1 tablespoon of oil, then tilt the pan to cover the entire base or use a brush to spread over the base of the pan.

4 Once hot, use a ¼ measuring cup (60ml) to scoop up a portion of the batter which should be more than enough for 2 blinis. Pour in 6-7 portions of the batter, depending on how big your pan is, and fry for 1 minute. Once the edges are starting to look less wet, flip and fry for a further 30-45 seconds. Transfer to a plate and repeat to use up all the batter.

5 Leave to cool before adding your topping of choice.

TIP Fancy making a larger amount of blinis as pictured? Simply double all of the ingredients. Fry as many as will comfortably fit in your pan at one time until you've used up all the batter. Ensure you stir the batter well between batches.

use carrot instead of onion, use gluten-free plain (all-purpose) flour instead of gram flour, and serve with a low FODMAP dip

---

- Vegetable oil, for frying
- 1 medium potato, peeled and grated or very thinly sliced
- 1 small onion, thinly sliced, or 1 small carrot, grated
- 1 small sweet potato, grated or very thinly sliced
- 4 tbsp frozen peas
- 1 tbsp garlic-infused oil
- 2 tsp mild curry powder
- ¼ tsp dried chilli flakes
- 2 tsp minced ginger paste
- ½ tsp ground turmeric
- 1 tsp dried fenugreek leaves
- Handful of fresh coriander (cilantro), roughly chopped
- ½ tsp salt
- ¼ tsp pepper
- 150g (1 cup plus 2 tbsp) gram flour or gluten-free plain (all-purpose) flour
- 100ml (½ cup minus 1½ tbsp) water
- Mango chutney, to serve

Pictured on page 80

CRISPY VEGGIE PAKORAS

Makes 12-13 ❄

Prep + Cook 30 mins

These little crispy nuggets of spiced, fried veggies are invited to every party at my house until the end of time. Prepping the veg is the part that's most time-consuming, so I often cheat and use my food processor with the grating attachment, which means I can make these in 15-20 minutes. My advice is to get the prep done ahead of time, then all that's left to do is mix and fry.

1 Pour vegetable oil into a large, heavy-based wok until around a third full. Place over a medium heat until it reaches 170°C (340°F). If you don't have a digital food thermometer, use the wooden spoon handle test (page 16). Line a large plate with kitchen paper, ready for later.

2 Place all the prepared veg in a large mixing bowl, followed by the frozen peas.

3 Add the garlic-infused oil, curry powder, chilli flakes, ginger paste, turmeric, fenugreek, fresh coriander, salt and pepper, and mix in well.

4 Lastly, add the flour and mix well once again, before adding the water. Mix until everything becomes a little more bound together and sticky.

5 Once the oil is hot enough, take 1 heaped tablespoon of the mixture and use another tablespoon to compact it into the spoon a little. Carefully lower it into the oil and repeat until there are 4-5 portions frying at once.

6 Fry for 4 minutes, or until crispy, then remove and transfer to the plate lined with kitchen paper to absorb excess oil. Repeat to use up all of the pakora mixture.

7 Serve with mango chutney as a dip.

use dairy-free milk

 use lactose-free milk

 use lactose-free milk and a low FODMAP sweet chilli sauce

 use dairy-free milk

 use dairy-free milk

- Vegetable oil, for frying
- 50g (1¾oz) beansprouts
- 50g (1¾oz) carrot, grated or thinly sliced
- 50g (1¾oz) white cabbage, thinly sliced
- 4 spring onions (scallions), sliced into long, thin strips
- 150ml (⅝ cup) milk
- 6 rice paper spring roll wrappers
- Sweet chilli sauce, to serve

Pictured on page 68

VEGETABLE SPRING ROLLS

Makes 6 ❄

Prep + Cook 30 mins

Rice paper wrappers are an easy alternative to wheat-based wrappers and, more often than not, you can easily find them in the world foods aisle of the supermarket. With a little frying, they go super-crispy and if dipped in milk instead of water, they turn a lovely golden brown when fried too. Get the rice wrappers and the rest is a doddle.

1 Pour vegetable oil into a large, heavy-based wok until around a third full. Place over a medium heat until it reaches 170°C (340°F). If you don't have a digital food thermometer, use the wooden spoon handle test (page 16).

2 Place all the veg in a large mixing bowl and mix. Pour the milk into a large shallow dish or dinner plate with a reasonable lip.

3 Take one sheet of rice paper and submerge it in the milk for 20 seconds or so. Then place the sheet on a wooden surface or large chopping board.

4 After 10-20 seconds, the sheet should be pliable and a little sticky. Spoon a heaped tablespoon of the veg around 1cm (½in) below the centre of the sheet. Use your hands to make the filling into more of a sausage shape around 6cm (2¼in) long and 2cm (¾in) thick.

5 Take the bottom of the rice paper wrapper and overlap the filling. Then roll it forwards into a sausage shape until halfway. Then stop. Fold in both ends so that they form a nice straight line on each side. Then keep on rolling until you have a nice, tightly rolled spring roll. Repeat with the remaining wrappers and veg.

6 Once the oil has reached the desired temperature, carefully lower 3 spring rolls at a time into the oil. They should just gently bubble and float on the top. Cook for about 5 minutes, turning them halfway, until golden brown. (They often like to float on one side more than the other, so I hold mine down with a pair of tongs until the paler side is sufficiently coloured.)

7 Remove from the oil with a slotted spoon and place on a wire rack set over a baking tray to drain.

8 Repeat to cook all the spring rolls and serve with the sweet chilli sauce for dipping.

use low FODMAP sweet chilli
sauce and serve no more than
40g (1½oz) of halloumi per
person

- Vegetable oil, for greasing
- 2 medium eggs, beaten
- 100g (3½oz) gluten-free
  breadcrumbs
- 1 tsp smoked paprika
- ¼ tsp cayenne pepper
- 450g (1lb) halloumi, cut into
  fries 1cm (½ in) thick
- Sweet chilli sauce, to serve

5-INGREDIENT HALLOUMI FRIES

Makes 12 ❄

Prep + Cook 20 mins

Halloumi fries are the instant crowd-pleaser that often most of the crowd didn't know they wanted. You only need 5 ingredients to make them and, best of all, you can easily make them in the oven or air fryer, which means there's no need to deep-fry them.

1 Preheat your oven to 200°C fan / 220°C / 425°F. Lightly grease a baking sheet and line with non-stick baking parchment.

2 Put the eggs in a medium bowl. Put the breadcrumbs, smoked paprika and cayenne pepper in another bowl and mix.

3 Place half the halloumi fries into the egg and mix around until well coated, then transfer to the breadcrumb bowl and mix around until completely coated on all sides – don't forget the ends too.

4 Transfer to the prepared baking sheet and repeat with the remaining halloumi fries.

5 Bake in the oven for 10 minutes, or until the breadcrumbs are golden and the fries are slightly squidgy.

6 Serve with the sweet chilli sauce as a dip. These are best enjoyed warm, so if not serving straight away, keep them warm in a low oven and ideally serve on a hot plate.

To cook in an air fryer

Preheat the air fryer to 200°C (400°F) and spray a little oil into the tray. Place as many halloumi fries in the air fryer basket as will fit without touching, then generously spray with oil. Cook for 10 minutes, or until the breadcrumbs are golden and crispy.

use dairy-free milk

 use lactose-free milk

 use lactose-free milk and maple syrup instead of honey

 use the dairy-free milk, replace the egg with ½ a mashed ripe banana and use maple syrup instead of honey

---

- 150g (1 cup plus 2 tbsp) gluten-free self-raising (self-rising) flour
- 5 tbsp caster (superfine) sugar
- ½ tsp gluten-free baking powder
- 250ml (1 cup) milk
- 1 medium egg
- 2 tsp vanilla extract
- Vegetable oil, ideally in a spray bottle

For the cinnamon sugar
- 40g (3 tbsp) caster (superfine) sugar
- 40g (3 tbsp) light brown sugar
- 1 tsp ground cinnamon

For the chocolate sauce
- 100g (3½oz) dark (bittersweet) chocolate
- 75ml (scant ⅓ cup) milk
- 2 tbsp honey or maple syrup

WAFFLE CHURRO DIPPERS

Serves 2 (makes 6–10) ❋
Prep + Cook 20 mins

Fancy churros without the need to deep-fry them? Well, great news: that's exactly what my waffle churro dippers are for! Simply create and slice the waffles, and roll in cinnamon sugar. When dipped in chocolate sauce, nobody would notice the difference!

1 Start heating up your waffle maker. All waffle makers vary on your instructions, so follow the instructions of your particular machine.

2 In a large mixing bowl, combine the flour, sugar and baking powder. In a jug (pitcher), beat together the milk, egg and vanilla extract.

3 Create a well in the flour and pour in the milk and egg mixture while whisking thoroughly. After 30 seconds of whisking, it should be nice and smooth.

4 Once your waffle maker has heated, spray with vegetable oil and pour in one measure of your batter. I pour in roughly 60ml (2fl oz) batter at a time using a ¼ measuring cup. Close the lid and cook for 3–4 minutes until consistently golden and crisp on the outside.

5 Cut each waffle into three long strips, then mix the cinnamon sugar ingredients on a large dinner plate. While still warm, roll each waffle strip on the plate until well-coated.

6 For the chocolate sauce, grab a small saucepan and place over a low heat. Add the dark chocolate, milk and honey or maple syrup and allow to melt. Stir until well combined and serve as a dip.

30 MINUTE (OR LESS) SWEET TREATS

If you follow me on Instagram, you'll know how much I love a good sweet treat or classic bake. But if you suddenly told me I had to make them all in 30 minutes, not only would I immediately have a little panic, but there are actually very few that I'd still be able to whip up without exceeding that time limit.

So I decided to create a chapter that includes all my favourite sweet treats and desserts that can be made in <u>30 minutes or less</u>; everything from familiar classics, quick cookies, microwave wonders and speedy seaside doughnuts, right up to chocolatey desserts and puddings that'll never let you down.

So now not only are they dangerously easy to eat, but they're also dangerously quick to make. You have been warned!

use dairy-free milk and ensure lemon curd is dairy-free

 use lactose-free milk

 use lactose-free milk

- 180ml (¾ cup) milk
- 2 tbsp lemon juice
- 130ml (½ cup plus 2 tsp) vegetable oil
- 1 large egg
- 200g (1 cup) caster (superfine) sugar
- 1 tsp bicarbonate of soda (baking soda)
- ¼ tsp xanthan gum
- 300g (2¼ cups) gluten-free self-raising (self-rising) flour
- Grated zest of 3 lemons
- 2½ tbsp poppy seeds
- 4 tbsp demerara or granulated sugar

To finish

- 100g (scant ¾ cup) icing (confectioners') sugar
- 4 tsp lemon juice
- Lemon curd (optional)

LEMON AND POPPY SEED MUFFINS

Makes 12 ❄

Prep 10 mins **+ Cook** 18–20 mins

Muffins are so often overlooked when people can pop into a bakery and choose whatever they like (obviously not us gf folk – the phrase 'we wish' suddenly comes to mind!). However, when they're this light and fluffy with a vibrant natural yellow hue and the perfect balance of sweet citrus flavour, these are simply too good to pass up. If you don't like poppy seeds, then feel free to leave them out, but they really do take these muffins up a notch.

1 Preheat your oven to 180°C fan / 200°C / 400°F. Line a 12-hole muffin tray with muffin or tulip cases.

2 Add the milk and lemon juice to a jug (pitcher) and allow to stand for 10 minutes until it curdles a little.

3 Add the oil, milk mixture and egg to a large mixing bowl. Whisk until combined and smooth. Next, add the caster sugar, bicarb, xanthan gum, flour, lemon zest and poppy seeds. Whisk until just combined then immediately stop mixing. Be gentle and don't over-whisk!

4 Divide the mixture evenly between the muffin cases and sprinkle the top of each with a pinch of demerara or granulated sugar.

5 Bake in the oven for 18–20 minutes until golden and a skewer inserted into the centre comes out clean. Remove from the oven and allow to cool.

6 Meanwhile, mix enough of the lemon juice with the icing sugar to create a fairly thick icing. Drizzle on top of each cooled muffin and add a dollop of lemon curd if you desire!

use dairy-free butter, chocolate chips and chocolate spread

 use lactose-free chocolate and chocolate spread

- 115g (½ cup) butter, softened
- 115g (½ cup plus 1 tbsp) light brown sugar
- 2 medium eggs, beaten
- 400–500g (15–18oz) overripe bananas, mashed
- 250g (1¾ cups plus 2 tbsp) gluten-free plain (all-purpose) flour
- ¼ tsp xanthan gum
- 1 tsp bicarbonate of soda (baking soda)
- 70g (2½oz) chocolate chips
- About 6 tbsp Nutella

Pictured on page 164

NUTELLA BANANA MUFFINS

Makes 12 ❄

Prep 10 mins **+ Cook** 20 mins

'**I've got loads of overripe bananas to use up, what do I do with them?!' is a phrase I have been asked weekly for years, so here's a scrummy suggestion for you. I also have a little rhyme to entice you further: 'Banana and Nutella, go well together.' Please don't bother making these until your bananas are really ripe, as unripe bananas simply won't do, so be patient if you can!**

1 Preheat your oven to 180°C fan / 200°C / 400°F. Line a 12-hole muffin tray with muffin cases.

2 In a large mixing bowl, cream together the butter and sugar until light and pale (I use an electric hand whisk or a stand mixer for this). Add the eggs and mashed banana and mix until well combined.

3 Add the flour, xanthan gum and bicarb and mix briefly until no dry flour can be seen. Lastly, add the chocolate chips and mix once more.

4 Spoon the mixture into your muffin cases, to come just under halfway up (don't use all the mixture yet). Add a heaped teaspoon of Nutella to the centre of each then spoon over more mixture to cover the Nutella.

5 Place a small amount of Nutella on the top of each muffin and use a skewer to swirl it all around, making a marbled swirly pattern.

6 Bake in the oven for 20–25 minutes until cooked through. Cool briefly in the tin before transferring to a wire rack to cool further. Enjoy warm or cold.

TIP You can make these as simple banana muffins without the Nutella, or swap the Nutella for peanut butter.

use dairy-free butter and chocolate

 use lactose-free chocolate

VE use dairy-free butter and chocolate

- 55g (2oz) popcorn (sweet, sweet and salty, or toffee)
- 45g (3½ tbsp) butter
- 115g (4oz) golden syrup
- 1 tsp vanilla extract
- 1 tbsp sesame seeds
- 1 heaped tbsp pumpkin seeds
- Dark (bittersweet) chocolate, melted (optional)

POPJACKS

Makes 6 ❄
Prep + Cook 10 mins

I've been meaning to share this recipe with you for a really long time – a tasty bar that has neither nuts or oats in it, it's a sticky popcorn bar that tastes like a buttery flapjack! These are perfect to take out with you for a snack on-the-go and the flavourings can be changed up to suit your own desires. For a chunkier bar just double the ingredients, though I quite like these as popcorn slabs!

1 Line a 20 x 20cm (8 x 8in) baking tin (pan) with non-stick baking parchment.

2 Crush the popcorn in your hands so the pieces are slightly smaller, but not too small!

3 In a small saucepan, melt the butter and golden syrup together and allow it to thicken a little.

4 Remove from the heat, add the vanilla extract and stir in the popcorn so it's well coated in the mixture.

5 Stir in the seeds and spread the mixture evenly into the tin. Pop in the fridge to chill briefly before removing from the tin. If you like, drizzle with melted chocolate and return to the fridge to set before cutting into bars.

TIP Swap in whatever seeds you'd like, or to change it up, use chocolate chips, dried fruit or chopped nuts.

use dairy-free butter

 use dairy-free butter and use a flax egg instead of the egg (see TIP below)

- 125g (4½oz) peanut butter (smooth or crunchy)
- 125g (½ cup plus 1 tbsp) unsalted butter, softened
- 110g (½ cup plus 1 tbsp) light brown sugar
- 110g (½ cup plus 1 tbsp) caster (superfine) sugar
- 1 large egg, beaten
- 2 tsp vanilla extract
- 225g (1¾ cups) gluten-free plain (all-purpose) flour
- ½ tsp gluten-free baking powder
- ¼ tsp xanthan gum
- Pinch of salt
- ½ tsp jam (jelly) per cookie

PB&J COOKIES

Makes 16-18 ❄

Prep + Cook 25 mins

So often, cookies need to be chilled before you bake them to prevent them from spreading too much. It's not a problem, but it does mean they don't stand a chance of being made in less than 30 minutes! However, these peanut butter and jam (jelly) cookies can be baked straight away and they'll spread to the perfect thickness, while still being super-soft and chewy.

1 Preheat your oven to 160°C fan / 180°C / 350°F. Line a couple of baking trays with non-stick baking parchment.

2 In a large bowl, mix together the peanut butter and butter, then add both sugars and cream together until fluffy. Add the egg and vanilla extract and mix once more to combine. Add the flour, baking powder, xanthan gum and salt. Mix until just combined into a soft but workable dough.

3 Roll the dough into 16-18 equal sized balls (mine are about 50g/1¾oz each). Use your thumb or a finger to press a dip into each ball, and spoon jam into the dip.

4 Place your balls well spaced out on the prepared baking trays and bake for about 12 minutes until golden, flattened and with a lovely jammy centre.

5 Allow to cool briefly on the baking tray before transferring to a wire rack to cool completely.

TIP If you're egg-free or vegan, a flax egg is a great substitute for eggs when making biscuits, cookies, muffins and pancakes. Simply combine 1 tbsp ground flaxseed with 3 tbsp of water in a small bowl. Allow to rest in the fridge for 15 minutes before using in place of one egg. Double or triple the quantities depending on how many eggs you're replacing.

use dairy-free milk, butter and chocolate chips

 use lactose-free milk and chocolate chips

 use lactose-free milk and chocolate chips

 use dairy-free milk, butter and chocolate chips

- 250g (2 cups minus 1 tbsp) gluten-free plain (all-purpose) flour
- 125g (½ cup plus 1 tbsp) butter, softened
- 100g (½ cup) caster (superfine) sugar
- 100g (½ cup) light brown sugar
- 2 tsp vanilla extract
- 2 tbsp milk
- 200g (7oz) chocolate chips

Optional dough extras
- Handful of mini marshmallows
- Extra chocolate chips

CHOC CHIP COOKIE DOUGH

Makes 20–25 balls ❄

Prep + Cook 15 mins

Say hello to my edible chocolate chip cookie dough. Wait... isn't all cookie dough edible?! Well it is, but fun fact: edible cookie dough isn't strictly safe to eat if it contains raw flour. Cooking the flour is a super-quick process though, and the resulting cookie dough can be enjoyed in so many different ways – to prove it, I've popped some serving suggestions below that I know you'll love.

1 Preheat your oven to 160°C fan / 180°C / 350°F.

2 Spread the flour out on a baking tray and bake in the oven for 8 minutes. Remove and allow to cool.

3 Cream together the butter and both sugars until light and fluffy.

4 Add the cooled flour and vanilla extract and mix in. Add the milk gradually and mix until it has the consistency you want – you may not need all the milk. Mix in your chocolate chips and any other extra additions.

5 Wrap in cling film (plastic wrap) and store in the fridge until you want to use it – for up to a week.

6 Enjoy on its own, alongside vanilla ice cream with a drizzling of caramel sauce. Or roll into mini balls to decorate your finished bakes or even as a filling for cupcakes. If you fancy, roll balls of cookie dough in melted chocolate and chill in the fridge to make cookie dough truffles.

use dairy-free milk, butter and chocolate chips

 use lactose-free milk and chocolate chips

 use lactose-free milk and chocolate chips

 use dairy-free milk, butter and chocolate chips, and a flax egg instead of the egg (see TIP on page 168)

- 220g (1¾ cups) gluten-free self-raising (self-rising) flour
- ¼ tsp xanthan gum
- 1 tsp gluten-free baking powder
- 110g (½ cup) cold butter, chopped
- 85g (7 tbsp) caster (superfine) sugar
- 110g (3¾oz) dark (bittersweet) chocolate chips
- 1 medium egg
- 1 tsp vanilla extract
- 1 tsp milk (optional)
- Demerara sugar, for sprinkling

CHOCOLATE CHIP ROCK CAKES

Makes 10 ❄

Prep + Cook 15 mins

I remember making rock cakes at a friend's house when I was about seven years old and being really excited to eat them, only to discover that they had dried fruit in them – not my favourite food as a fussy child! However, I soon realized that you could make them with chocolate chips, and it was a game changer for me!

1 Preheat your oven to 180°C fan / 200°C / 400°F. Line a large baking tray with non-stick baking parchment.

2 Place the flour, xanthan gum and baking powder in large mixing bowl. Add the cold butter and rub it in with your fingertips to a fine breadcrumb consistency. Stir in the caster sugar and chocolate chips.

3 Crack in your egg and vanilla extract and mix until the mixture comes together into a thick dough. If it's a little dry, add a teaspoon of milk at a time, but only if you need to; you don't want it too wet or the rock cakes will spread too much.

4 Place spoonfuls of the dough mixture on your prepared baking tray with a decent gap between them, as they will spread. You don't need to round them off; messy balls are fine as they come out more rock-like!

5 Sprinkle each with a tiny amount of demerara sugar (for added texture) and bake in the oven for 15–20 minutes until golden and cooked through.

6 Allow to cool briefly on the baking tray before moving to a cooling rack to finish cooling. Enjoy cold or still slightly warm.

TIP Prefer more traditional rock cakes? Simply switch the chocolate chips for dried fruit, or for a twist, add some grated marzipan.

use dairy-free butter and milk, and ensure fillings are dairy-free

 use lactose-free milk and ensure fillings are lactose-free

 follow the low lactose advice

 use dairy-free butter, use a flax egg instead of the egg (see TIP on page 168), and ensure fillings are vegan-friendly

---

- 100g (½ cup minus 1 tbsp) butter, softened
- 100g (½ cup) caster (superfine) sugar
- 1 medium or large egg, beaten
- 1½ tsp vanilla extract
- 270g (2 cups) gluten-free plain (all-purpose) flour
- ½ tsp xanthan gum
- 20g (3 tbsp) unsweetened cocoa powder
- 1 tbsp milk

Filling suggestions (optional)
- Marshmallow fluff and jam (jelly)
- Chocolate spread
- Dulce de leche
- Peanut butter

MARBLE BISCUITS

Makes 20 (or 10 biscuit sandwiches) ❄

Prep + Cook 25 mins

I love an accidental bake, which these biscuits certainly are! I first made them when I was testing out my pinwheel cookies in *How to Bake Anything Gluten Free* - I had some leftover chocolate and vanilla dough that I pushed together and, just like that, a new biscuit was born! The recipe has developed since then and I've also found that sandwiching them together with a little marshmallow fluff and jam (jelly) is the best finishing touch.

1 Preheat your oven to 170°C fan / 190°C / 375°F. Line two baking trays with non-stick baking parchment.

2 In a large mixing bowl, cream together the butter and sugar until light and fluffy.

3 Add the egg and vanilla extract, and briefly mix in. Next, add the flour and xanthan gum and mix until all the flour is incorporated and it starts to come together as a dough.

4 Split your dough in half (slightly more in one bowl than the other). Sift the cocoa powder and add the milk to the bowl with slightly less dough in it. Mix together until uniformly brown.

5 Tear both the vanilla and chocolate balls of dough into smaller pieces and then push them all together into a single ball of dough that is a mix of chocolate and vanilla colours.

6 Roll the dough out to about 6mm (¼in) in thickness, creating a marbled dough. Cut out your shapes - any shapes or sizes. Mine were 5.5cm (2¼in) circles but feel free to cut out stars, hearts, etc.

7 Place on the prepared baking trays - they shouldn't spread so they can be quite close together. Bake for 8-10 minutes, bearing in mind that larger cookies may need a little longer and smaller ones a little less.

8 Allow to cool briefly on the tray before transferring to a wire rack to cool completely.

9 Enjoy as they are, ice them or, if you want to make biscuit sandwiches, spread your filling of choice into the centre of one of the biscuits and sandwich with a second.

use dairy-free chocolate spread

 use lactose-free chocolate spread

 use lactose-free chocolate spread

 use dairy-free chocolate spread and brush with dairy-free milk instead of egg

---

- 280g (10oz) store-bought gluten-free puff pastry (see TIP if using homemade)
- 90g (3¼oz) Nutella
- 1 egg, beaten
- Icing (confectioners') sugar, for dusting

4-INGREDIENT CHOCOLATE TWISTS

Makes 5 ❄

Prep 5 mins **+ Cook** 15 mins

When I was 16, I worked in my local supermarket, which had a fab bakery at the back. Near the end of each shift, all baked goods were reduced and then those not sold were disposed of at the end of the day. I simply couldn't allow the chocolate twists to go to waste, so I'd always take one home and have it for my 10pm dinner, believe it or not! I wouldn't be able to do that these days, so instead I make my own using just four simple ingredients.

1 Preheat your oven to 200°C fan / 220°C / 425°F. Line a baking tray with non-stick baking parchment.

2 Unroll the pastry, cut it in half and spread one half with Nutella, then place the other half of pastry on top of it, like a sandwich.

3 Cut the pastry into 5 equal sections about 2.5cm (1in) wide. Hold each end of a strip and twist, then place on the baking sheet. Repeat with the remaining strips.

4 Brush all over with egg and bake in the oven for 15 minutes, covering them loosely with foil after 10 minutes so they don't get too crisp or brown. Remove and allow to cool a little before dusting with icing sugar and enjoying.

TIP Sprinkle some chopped hazelnuts on top of the Nutella, for extra crunch. If using homemade gluten-free rough puff pastry (see the recipe in my first or second books), simply roll out to a 20 x 30cm (8 x 12in) rectangle 3mm (⅛in) thick, and proceed as directed above.

brush with dairy-free milk
instead of egg

- 200g (7oz) apple pie filling from
  a can
- ¾ tsp ground cinnamon
- ¼ tsp grated nutmeg
- 280g (10oz) store-bought
  gluten-free puff pastry
  (see TIP if using homemade)
- 1 egg, beaten
- Demerara sugar, for sprinkling

QUICK APPLE TURNOVER PIES

Makes 4 ❄

Prep + Cook 25 mins

Apple turnovers from the supermarket bakery and McDonald's
apple pies were two things I adored growing up. So to suddenly
be told I couldn't have them anymore, ever, was an absolute kick
in the teeth that I still haven't quite got over. Fortunately, these
apple turnover pies pay homage to those two items and are so
easy to create using store-bought gluten-free pastry and apple
pie filling.

1 Preheat your oven to 200°C fan / 220°C / 425°F. Line a baking
tray with non-stick baking parchment.

2 Mix the apple pie filling with the cinnamon and nutmeg.

3 Cut the pastry sheet into 8 evenly sized rectangles. Spoon a couple
of teaspoons of the apple mixture into the centre of one rectangle,
leaving about a 1cm (½in) border around the edges. Brush the border
with beaten egg and place another sheet of pastry on top. Seal with
a fork and repeat to make 4 apple-filled parcels.

4 Place on the prepared baking sheet and brush all over with egg.
Cut two small slits in the top of each with a sharp knife and sprinkle
with demerara sugar.

5 Bake for 15–20 minutes until puffed up and golden, covering loosely
with foil after 12–14 minutes if they are browning too fast.

6 Remove from the oven and allow to cool very briefly, then enjoy hot
(my preferred choice) or cold... with custard, or without!

TIP You can fill these with other fruit fillings or even add in a little
caramel sauce to the apple to make caramel apple pies. If using
homemade gluten-free rough puff pastry (see the recipe in my first
or second books), simply roll out to a 20 x 30cm (8 x 12in) rectangle
3mm (⅛in) thick, and proceed as directed above.

use water instead of milk

 use lactose-free milk

 use lactose-free milk and serve with maple syrup

 use water instead of milk

- Vegetable oil, for frying
- 1 x 425g (15oz) can of pineapple rings in syrup or juice
- 4 tbsp gluten-free plain (all-purpose) flour
- Golden syrup, to serve

For the batter
- 100g (¾ cup) gluten-free plain (all-purpose) flour
- ½ tsp gluten-free baking powder
- 120ml (½ cup) milk or water

PINEAPPLE FRITTERS

Makes 8 (serves 2-4) ❄

Prep 5 mins **+ Cook** 15 mins

Wherever we used to go on family holidays, it didn't matter where we were in the world, we'd always end up finding a Chinese restaurant and I'd always finish my dinner with some sort of fruit fritter. Pineapple fritters not only taste amazing but they also look a bit like doughnuts, which makes them even better. And by using golden syrup to drizzle you'll be enjoying these in no time!

1 Add enough vegetable oil to a large, heavy-based wok until about one-third full. Place over a medium heat until it reaches 170°C (340°F). If you don't have a digital food thermometer, use the wooden spoon handle test (page 16). Line a large plate with kitchen paper, ready for later.

2 Drain the pineapple rings of all their syrup or juice, and leave in the can for now. Spread the flour out on a large dinner plate.

3 In a large mixing bowl, combine the ingredients for the batter and whisk together until smooth and consistent.

4 Take 3 pineapple rings at a time and place them on the flour plate, ensuring coverage on both sides and the edges.

5 Once the oil is hot enough, dredge each ring in the batter; be careful as they're quite delicate, but don't worry if some break. Once coated, carefully lower into the hot oil – I find using a small pair of tongs easiest.

6 Cook for 2–3 minutes until golden on both sides. Once golden, transfer to the plate lined with kitchen paper to drain. Repeat to cook the remaining pineapple rings.

7 Serve with a generous drizzling of golden syrup.

TIP If you've frozen these, simply defrost in the fridge and bake in a hot oven until crisp.

use dairy-free butter and milk

 use lactose-free milk

 use lactose-free milk

 use dairy-free butter and milk, and use 6 tbsp aquafaba (whisked until frothy) instead of the eggs

---

- 100g (½ cup minus 1 tbsp) butter, softened, plus extra for greasing
- 100g (½ cup) caster (superfine) sugar
- 2 medium eggs
- ½ tsp almond extract
- 80g (⅔ cup minus 1 tbsp) gluten-free self-raising (self-rising) flour
- 20g (¾oz) ground almonds
- 1 tsp milk
- 3–4 tsp raspberry or cherry jam (jelly), plus extra to serve
- Toasted flaked (slivered) almonds

BAKEWELL MICROWAVE PUDDINGS

Serves 3-4

Prep + Cook 7 mins

As I'm a big Bakewell tart fan, I'm also, not surprisingly, the sort of person who craves Bakewell flavours in places you'd never expect. So if you are too, then this is definitely the pud for you! Finish this one off with more hot jam (jelly), a sprinkling of toasted flaked (slivered) almonds and, of course, plenty of custard.

1 Butter 3 or 4 small ramekin dishes, each about 10cm (4in) in diameter.

2 Add all the ingredients except the jam and flaked almonds to a bowl and mix together for about a minute.

3 Spread a teaspoon of jam into the bottom of each ramekin then spoon your mixture on top of it. It should go about halfway up the ramekin.

4 Cover each ramekin with a little cling film (plastic wrap) and pierce the top a few times.

5 Place in the microwave on high at 900W for about 90 seconds. Allow to sit for 30 seconds or so then turn out onto a plate.

6 Finish with extra jam and toasted flaked almonds. Enjoy with custard.

TIP You can make one large pudding to serve 4, in a bigger microwavable dish, and cook for around 3 minutes. Or you can halve the amount if you just want 1 or 2 puddings.

use dairy-free butter and lemon curd

 use lactose-free milk

 use lactose-free milk

 use dairy-free butter and lemon curd, and use 6 tbsp aquafaba (whisked until frothy) instead of the eggs

---

- 100g (½ cup minus 1 tbsp) butter, softened, plus extra for greasing
- 100g (½ cup) caster (superfine) sugar
- 100g (¾ cup) gluten-free self-raising (self-rising) flour
- 2 medium eggs
- Grated zest of 2 lemons
- 1 tsp lemon juice
- 3–4 tbsp lemon curd, hot

LEMON CURD MICROWAVE PUDDINGS

Serves 3–4

Prep + Cook 7 mins

This speedy pud will leave lemon fans more than satisfied, and if you have any guests knocking on the door unexpectedly, you can get this done from start to finish in less than 10 minutes. Make sure you allow the lemon curd to slightly cool before taking a mouthful, unless you're a fan of molten hot lemon curd lava! Don't forget with this recipe, as with my Bakewell puds opposite, you can always make one big pudding instead of 3–4 little ones; check the TIP for how to do so.

1 Butter 3 or 4 small ramekin dishes, each about 10cm (4in) in diameter.

2 Add all the ingredients except the lemon curd to a bowl and mix together for about a minute.

3 Spoon your mixture evenly into the ramekins – it should come about halfway up them.

4 Cover with cling film (plastic wrap), poke a few holes in the top and place in the microwave on high at 900W for about 90 seconds. Leave for a minute or so before turning out onto a plate and topping each with hot lemon curd.

5 Serve up with custard, cream or ice cream.

TIP You can make one large pudding to serve 4, in a bigger microwavable dish, and cook for around 3 minutes. Or you can halve the amount if you just want 1 or 2 puddings.

use dairy-free butter and chocolate

 use lactose-free chocolate

 use lactose-free chocolate

 use dairy-free butter and chocolate, and use 9 tbsp aquafaba (whisked until frothy) instead of the eggs

---

- 150g (⅔ cup) butter, plus extra for greasing
- 200g (7oz) milk or dark (bittersweet) chocolate – I use half and half
- 150g (¾ cup) caster (superfine) sugar
- 3 large eggs
- 40g (5 tbsp) gluten-free plain (all-purpose) flour
- 10g (1½ tbsp) unsweetened cocoa powder

HOT CHOCOLATE POTS

Makes 6 ❄

Prep + Cook 20 mins

When you're questioning what to make for a quick dessert, these hot chocolate pots should always be the answer. They only take 15 minutes in the oven and what emerges is a gooey, chocolatey heaven beneath a slightly crisp top. Don't forget to finish it off with a scoop of vanilla ice cream!

1 Preheat your oven to 180°C fan / 200°C / 400°F. Grease 6 ramekin dishes, each about 10cm (4in) in diameter, with a little butter.

2 Melt together the chocolate and butter in the microwave – do this in short bursts, stirring in between.

3 In a large mixing bowl, whisk together the sugar and eggs until frothy.

4 Add the melted chocolate and butter mixture to the sugar and eggs and fold it in. Fold in the flour and cocoa powder carefully until combined.

5 Fill each of your ramekins so they are about three-quarters full. Bake in the oven for 12–15 minutes (it varies depending on the size of your ramekins) until risen and possibly with a slight crack on top.

6 Remove from the oven and serve warm, ideally with a scoop of ice cream.

TIP You can chill the filled ramekins in the fridge before baking (or freeze them), allowing you to make these ahead of time. Allow an extra 2 minutes in the oven if cooking from chilled, and 5 minutes if from frozen. Ensure you use metal, non-stick ramekins if freezing.

use dairy-free milk and chocolate chips

 use lactose-free milk and chocolate chips

 use lactose-free milk and chocolate chips

 use dairy-free milk and chocolate chips

- 1 tbsp vegetable oil
- 4 tbsp milk
- 2 tbsp caster (superfine) sugar
- 1 tbsp unsweetened cocoa powder
- 3 tbsp gluten-free plain (all-purpose) flour
- ½ tsp gluten-free baking powder
- 1 tbsp chocolate chips

CHOCOLATE MUG CAKE

Serves 1
Prep + Cook 5 mins

This comforting little mug cake is all you need when you fancy a light and fluffy chocolate chip sponge pudding but can't really manage a full-on baking session. Better still, there's barely any washing up involved as you mix the ingredients together in the mug you'll be eating it from. This amount makes one mug's worth, so if you want to make more than one, just scale up the quantities.

1 Add all the ingredients to a microwavable mug and mix together with a fork to combine fully.

2 Cover with cling film (plastic wrap), poke a few holes in the top and microwave on high at 900W for about 60–70 seconds.

3 Allow to sit for about a minute before enjoying as it is, or topping with a scoop of ice cream and some chocolate sauce.

use dairy-free milk

 use lactose-free milk

 use lactose-free milk

- 2 tbsp caster (superfine) sugar, plus extra to serve
- ¼ tsp ground cinnamon, plus extra to serve
- 2 tbsp vegetable oil
- 1 large egg yolk
- 1 tbsp milk
- ¼ tsp vanilla extract
- 4 tbsp gluten-free plain (all-purpose) flour
- ½ tsp gluten-free baking powder
- 2 tsp jam (jelly) of your choice, plus extra to serve

JAM DOUGHNUT MUG CAKE

Serves 1

Prep + Cook 5 mins

I will take any opportunity to make something doughnut related and this is no exception. This is a proper hug in a mug with a sticky jammy centre and a crunchy sugary finish. And, best of all, once you've mixed everything together you'll be ready to indulge in approximately one minute. On your marks, get set... microwave!

1 Add all the ingredients except the jam to a microwavable mug and mix together with a fork to combine fully.

2 Spoon the jam into the centre, cover with cling film (plastic wrap), poke a few holes in the top and microwave on high at 900W for about 60–70 seconds.

3 Allow to sit for about a minute before topping with a little extra cinnamon sugar (mix cinnamon and caster sugar together) and extra jam if needed!

use dairy-free butter and a dairy-free yoghurt instead of sour cream

 use lactose-free yoghurt instead of sour cream

 use lactose-free yoghurt instead of sour cream

- Vegetable oil, for frying
- 25g (2 tbsp) butter, softened
- 20g (1½ tbsp) caster (superfine) sugar, plus extra for coating
- 30g (2 tbsp) light brown sugar
- 1 large egg yolk
- ½ tsp vanilla extract
- 80g (3oz) sour cream
- 130g (1 cup) gluten-free self-raising (self-rising) flour, plus extra for dusting
- ¼ tsp xanthan gum
- ½ tbsp cornflour (cornstarch)
- ¼ tsp grated nutmeg (optional)

SEASIDE DOUGHNUTS

Makes 12–15 ❄

Prep + Cook 25 mins

I couldn't make a quick and easy cookbook without giving you a doughnut recipe, and this one is super-special. Remember those hot sugared doughnuts in a paper bag you could get at the seaside, a funfair or a market?! Well this is them... but gluten-free! A food thermometer is super-handy for frying these, and once you get the hang of it, you won't want to stop making them.

1 Half-fill a large, deep, heavy-based saucepan with vegetable oil and place over a medium heat until it reaches 170°C (340°F). If you don't have a digital food thermometer, use the wooden spoon handle test (page 16).

2 Meanwhile, in a large mixing bowl, cream together the butter and sugars until light and fluffy. Add the egg yolk and vanilla extract and mix in until combined, then stir in the sour cream, ensuring it's fully incorporated.

3 In a medium mixing bowl, mix together the flour, xanthan gum, cornflour and nutmeg, if using, then add them to your bowl of wet ingredients. Mix by hand with a spatula so you don't overmix. The dough will be a little sticky but not unmanageable.

4 On a lightly floured surface and with floured hands roll the dough out carefully to around 2cm (¾in) thick and use a 6cm (2½in) plain round cutter to cut out your doughnuts, and a 2cm (¾in) round cutter to remove a hole from the middle.

5 Once the oil is hot enough, lower the doughnuts into it in batches of 3 – they should sizzle gently and float. Fry for around 1½–2 minutes on each side until golden, then remove from the oil using a slotted spoon and place on a plate lined with kitchen paper to absorb excess oil. Repeat with the rest of your doughnuts.

6 Place the warm doughnuts on a plate of sugar to coat all over, then transfer to a wire rack to cool a little, although they are best served warm just like when you have them at the seaside!

TIP You can keep this dough in the fridge before you roll it out, which will make it even more manageable, but is not necessary. Also, instead of rolling it out you can roll it into balls with no hole in the middle – they will take a similar time to cook as the rings.

use dairy-free milk and butter

 use lactose-free milk

 use lactose-free milk; 2 Welsh cakes is a safe low FODMAP serving size

 use dairy-free milk and butter and a flax egg instead of the egg (see TIP on page 168)

- 220g (1¾ cups) gluten-free plain (all-purpose) flour, plus extra for dusting
- ½ tsp xanthan gum
- 1 tsp gluten-free baking powder
- 1 tsp ground mixed spice
- 75g (6 tbsp) caster (superfine) sugar
- 100g (½ cup minus 1 tbsp) cold butter, cubed, plus extra for greasing
- 75g (2½oz) currants
- 1 medium or large egg, beaten
- 1 tsp milk

WELSH CAKES

Makes 12–14 ❄

Prep + Cook 25 mins

I can't say Welsh cakes were something I ever ate prior to going gluten-free, but the number of requests I've had for a recipe over the years totally intrigued me to the point that this recipe now exists! They really are so quick to rustle up, melt-in-the-mouth delicious, and certainly not just for St David's Day!

1 Place the flour, xanthan gum, baking powder, mixed spice and sugar in a large bowl and mix together.

2 Add the cold cubed butter and rub it in with your fingertips until the mixture resembles breadcrumbs.

3 Stir in the currants until evenly dispersed.

4 Gradually add the beaten egg, working it in using a fork so that the mixture starts to come together. Add the milk to help bring it together more, like a dough. You don't want the dough to be dry, so add a little extra milk if you need to.

5 Flour your work surface and roll out your dough to about 6–8mm (¼–⅓in) thick. If the dough is sticky, just flour the top of the dough and your rolling pin.

6 Use a round cookie cutter about 6cm (2¼in) in diameter and cut circles out of the dough.

7 Heat up a frying pan or skillet over a medium heat and grease with a little butter or oil. Add a few of the Welsh cakes and cook for 2½–3 minutes on each side until lovely and golden on both sides.

8 Remove from the pan and repeat to cook the remaining cakes.

9 Serve warm or cold, sprinkled with a little caster sugar, or with some butter and jam.

LAZY CLASSICS + NO-BAKE DESSERTS

Welcome to the ultimate selection of lazy bakes and no-bake desserts. Much like the lazy comfort food chapter, these recipes ask for just 15–20 minutes of effort, then you either bake them in the oven or chill in the fridge, and voilà – they're done.

So yes, these recipes take longer than 30 minutes, but it was absolutely integral they went into this book as they actually require less hands-on effort than lots of the 30-minute recipes.

I've crammed this chapter with tons of classics, with everything from mint chocolate slices, to a doughnut celebration cake, fridge cake, right up to classics like Yorkshire parkin cake, school dinner sponge cake, pineapple upside down cake and more.

use dairy-free butter, white chocolate, cream cheese (minimum 23% fat) and cream (minimum 30% fat)

 use lactose-free white chocolate, cream cheese and lactose-free whipping cream (minimum 30% fat)

 use lactose-free white chocolate, cream cheese and lactose-free whipping cream (minimum 30% fat)

 use dairy-free butter, white chocolate, cream cheese (minimum 23% fat) and cream (minimum 30% fat)

- 500g (1lb 2oz) mascarpone
- 100g (scant ¾ cup) icing (confectioners') sugar
- ½ tsp vanilla extract
- 300ml (1¼ cups) double (heavy) cream
- 250g (9oz) white chocolate, melted and just cooled, plus extra chunks to decorate
- 275g (10oz) fresh raspberries, plus extra to decorate

For the base

- 320g (11oz) gluten-free digestive biscuits (graham crackers)
- 150g (⅔ cup) butter, melted

WHITE CHOCOLATE AND RASPBERRY NO-BAKE CHEESECAKE

Serves 12–15 ❄

Prep 20 mins + **Chill** 5 hours (or overnight)

I put before you one of the greatest flavour combinations known to man. It's so simple, but white chocolate and raspberry go fabulously together, and in cheesecake form there's nothing better. You really can't beat a no-bake cheesecake for an easy dessert, and this one can be enjoyed all year round.

1 First, make your base. In a food processor, blitz the digestive biscuits to a crumb-like texture (or pop into a zip-lock bag and bash them with a rolling pin). Add to a large bowl and pour in your melted butter. Mix well. Spoon the mixture into a round 20cm (8in) loose-bottomed or springform tin (pan). Compact it into the base in an even layer, then chill in the fridge while you make your filling.

2 I use a stand mixer to make the filling, but you can easily do this using an electric hand whisk, or even by hand. Place the mascarpone, icing sugar and vanilla extract in the bowl of the stand mixer. Mix on a low to medium speed for 10–20 seconds, then add the cream. At a medium speed, mix for 2 more minutes, or until it begins to firm up.

3 Pour in the melted white chocolate and briefly mix until combined. Do not overmix as the mixture can split. It should end up as a nice, thick, spoonable consistency, not a pourable one. Gently fold in your raspberries until evenly dispersed. Spread your filling evenly on top of the chilled biscuit base and place in the fridge to chill for at least 5 hours, but ideally overnight.

4 When ready to serve, carefully remove from the tin and transfer to a serving plate. Decorate with extra fresh raspberries and chunks of white chocolate.

TIP Cheesecake in a hurry? Reduce the mixture and use individual ramekins. These will take a lot less time to chill. If freezing, simply add the decoration once defrosted.

use dairy-free butter, chocolate and cream (minimum 30% fat)

 use lactose-free whipping cream (minimum 30% fat) and chocolate

 use lactose-free whipping cream (minimum 30% fat) and chocolate

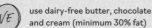 use dairy-free butter, chocolate and cream (minimum 30% fat)

For the base
- 350g (12oz) gluten-free digestive biscuits (graham crackers)
- 2 tbsp unsweetened cocoa powder
- 150g (⅔ cup) butter, melted

For the filling
- 300ml (1¼ cups) double (heavy) cream
- 300g (10½oz) chocolate (I use half dark/bittersweet and half milk), broken into pieces
- 55g (4 tbsp) butter

To finish
- 200ml (¾ cup plus 1½ tbsp) double (heavy) cream
- 1 tbsp icing (confectioners') sugar
- Chocolate, for grating

NO-BAKE CHOCOLATE CREAM PIE

Serves 12 ❄

Prep 20 mins **+ Chill** 3 hours

Gimme a buttery biscuit base, gimme a chocolate ganache, gimme whipped cream. What have you got?! You've got my No-Bake Chocolate Cream Pie. The layers in this dessert combine to create something really special – both in terms of flavour and texture – that I guarantee nobody will think it was easy to make. Pretend it wasn't, pretend you worked hard on it all day, make them feel special! When really you just spent 20 minutes on it and had the rest of the day to yourself... Nobody needs to know that bit!!

1 Crush the biscuits into fine crumbs in a food processor (or place in a zip-lock bag and bash with a rolling pin), then mix in the cocoa powder until thoroughly combined. Add to a large bowl and pour in your melted butter. Mix well. Press into the base and sides of a 23cm (9in) loose-bottomed fluted tart tin (pan) and chill in the freezer for 20 minutes, or a little longer in the fridge.

2 For the filling, heat the cream in a saucepan until just boiling. Remove from the heat and add the chocolate and butter. Stir continuously until it's all melted, combined and creamy. Pour over the chilled base and place back in the fridge until set.

3 Finish by whipping the cream to soft peaks. Fold in the icing sugar and spoon it on top of the chocolate layer. Sprinkle some grated chocolate on top to finish.

TIP you can also add a teaspoon of orange extract or mint extract to the filling mixture. The cream layer is optional – if freezing, only add the cream layer once defrosted.

use a dairy-free hard butter

- 300g (2¼ cups) gluten-free plain (all-purpose) flour
- 1½ tsp xanthan gum
- 145g (⅔ cup) very cold butter, cut into 1cm (½in) cubes
- 3 tbsp caster (superfine) sugar (for sweet pastry only)
- 1 tsp salt (for savoury pastry only)
- 2 large eggs, beaten

ULTIMATE, EASY SHORTCRUST PASTRY

Makes 560g (1lb 4oz) ❋

Prep 15 mins + **Chill** 30 mins

I thought I'd pop this one in not only to help you all out with the cornflake tart opposite, but also because this is my favourite gluten-free pastry recipe. It's so easy to work with that you'll forget about all those failed gluten-free pastry attempts in an instant. This is a great pastry for both sweet and savoury dishes, lots of which you'll find in my other books and on the blog too!

1 In a large mixing bowl, mix together the flour and xanthan gum. Make sure your butter is really cold; if not, put it in the fridge or freezer until nicely chilled. Add the cubes to the bowl and, using your fingertips, rub the butter into the flour until it has a breadcrumb-like consistency. Make sure your hands are cool, as we want to avoid the butter getting warm! (You can also achieve the same result by using a food processor to blitz the ingredients together.)

2 If making sweet pastry, stir in the sugar, or if making savoury pastry, stir in the salt.

3 Add your beaten egg and, using a knife, carefully cut it into the mixture until it comes together. It should form a ball and not be crumbly – it will be a little sticky to touch but not unmanageable.

4 Wrap the dough in cling film (plastic wrap) and leave to chill in the fridge for around 30 minutes before using. You can freeze this pastry for up to 2 months; defrost fully before using.

TIP Chill! Using cold butter and chilling the dough makes your gluten-free pastry stronger and more workable. Making any type of pastry on an incredibly hot day isn't advisable as the warmer your dough is, the more fragile it will become. However, make sure once chilled, you allow your pastry to warm up a bit before rolling, otherwise it will crack.

use dairy-free butter and pastry

 LL

 V

 use dairy free butter and vegan pastry

- 400g (14oz) store-bought gluten-free shortcrust pastry (or 1 quantity ultimate, easy shortcrust pastry, opposite)
- Gluten-free plain (all-purpose) flour, for dusting
- 50g (3½ tbsp) butter
- 125g (4½oz) golden syrup
- 25g (2 tbsp) light brown sugar
- 100g (3½oz) gluten-free cornflakes
- 100g (3½oz) strawberry jam (jelly), or whatever flavour you prefer

Pictured overleaf

CORNFLAKE TART

Serves 12 ❄

Prep 20 mins **+ Cook** 30 mins

A school dinner classic, hey? I actually never once had this at school, and the first time I had it I was in my mid-twenties! Now, I loved my primary school but I feel like we were thoroughly deprived, having never had this for pudding even once! Whether or not you've had cornflake tart before, you've got to try my recipe. The jammy cornflake filling bakes in 5 minutes and you can use shop-bought pastry or my recipe – both give fab results.

1 If your chilled pastry dough is quite firm, leaving it out at room temperature ahead of time is definitely advised. Lightly flour your rolling pin and a large sheet of non-stick baking parchment, then roll out the pastry on the parchment to a 2mm (⅟₁₆in) thickness. Aim for a large circular shape, but remember not to handle your dough excessively as this will warm it up and make it more fragile.

2 Transfer the pastry to a 23cm (9in) loose-bottomed fluted tart tin (pan) – I do this by supporting the pastry as I gently invert it into the tin, with equal overhang on all sides. Peel off the baking parchment.

3 Next, use your fingers to carefully ease the pastry into place, so that it neatly lines the tin. Lift the overhanging pastry and, using your thumb, squash 2mm (⅟₁₆in) of pastry back into the tin. This will result in slightly thicker sides which will prevent your pastry from shrinking when baked. Allow the overhang to do its thing – we'll trim it after chilling. Lightly prick the base of the pastry case several times with a fork then place in the fridge for 15 minutes. Meanwhile, preheat your oven to 180°C fan / 200°C / 400°F.

4 Remove the pastry case from the fridge and use a rolling pin to roll over the top of the tin, removing the overhang and flattening the pastry rim. Loosely line the base with a piece of scrunched up baking parchment and fill with baking beans (or uncooked rice if you don't have any). Place on a hot baking tray in the oven and bake for 15 minutes, then remove the baking parchment and baking beans and bake for a further 5 minutes.

5 In a saucepan, heat together your butter, golden syrup and sugar until melted and combined. Tip in the cornflakes and stir so they are coated in the mixture. Spread jam all over the base of your baked pastry case, then spoon the cornflake mixture on top of the jam.

6 Bake for 5–10 minutes until the cornflakes are lightly toasted. Allow to cool then serve warm, with custard.

use dairy-free butter

- 400g (1¾ cups) butter, softened
- 350g (1¾ cups) caster (superfine) sugar
- 6 large eggs
- 2 tsp vanilla extract
- 400g (3 cups) gluten-free self-raising (self-rising) flour
- ¼ tsp xanthan gum

For the icing
- 400g (3 cups) icing (confectioners') sugar
- 1 tsp vanilla extract
- Gluten-free sprinkles

SCHOOL DINNER SPONGE CAKE

Serves 12-15 ❉

Prep 20 mins **+ Cook** 55 mins

Now, this is a school dinner pudding I remember having on a regular basis and loving. A vanilla sponge with icing and sprinkles served with custard! It's actually been one of the most popular recipes on the blog for a very long time so I thought I'd sneak it into the book; it deserves it! While nothing beats having this with custard for dessert, it's also great to enjoy as cake, and it makes the perfect quick vanilla birthday cake with a no-fuss icing for a big party.

1 Preheat your oven to 160°C fan / 180°C / 350°F. Line a 23 x 33cm (9 x 13in) baking tin (pan) with non-stick baking parchment.

2 In a large mixing bowl, cream the butter and sugar until light and fluffy. Add the eggs one at a time, mixing between each addition. Add the vanilla extract and mix that in too, then add the flour and xanthan gum and mix until well combined.

3 Spoon/pour your mixture evenly into the baking tin and bake in the oven for 50-55 minutes until fully cooked and golden. Allow the cake to cool completely in the tin before lifting it out.

4 While the cake is cooling, make your icing. Sift the icing sugar into a large mixing bowl. Add the vanilla extract and very gradually add enough water, 1 tablespoon at a time, to achieve a thick, glossy icing. Sift in a little extra icing sugar if it seems too runny.

5 Spoon the icing over your cooled sponge, covering the top all the way to the edges. Scatter with colourful sprinkles and allow to fully set before cutting into squares.

TIP Have fun with the icing and add a little food colouring to make it even brighter! You can also change the flavour of the extract in both the icing and the cake.

use dairy-free butter, milk and chocolate

 use lactose-free milk and chocolate

 use lactose-free milk and chocolate

- 300g (1⅓ cups) butter, plus extra, softened, for greasing
- 300g (1½ cups) caster (superfine) sugar
- 5 medium eggs
- 225g (1¾ cups) gluten-free self-raising (self-rising) flour
- ¼ tsp xanthan gum
- 1 tsp gluten-free baking powder
- 140g (5oz) ground almonds
- 165ml (⅔ cup) milk
- 40g (1½oz) unsweetened cocoa powder
- 100g (3½oz) chocolate chips

For the icing
- 55g (¼ cup) butter
- 75g (2½oz) dark (bittersweet) chocolate
- 100g (scant ¾ cup) icing (confectioners') sugar, sifted
- Gluten-free sprinkles

CHOCOLATE DOUGHNUT CELEBRATION CAKE

Serves 12-15 ❉
Prep 20 mins **+ Cook** 55 mins

You know I said earlier I like to sneak in doughnut-related bakes wherever I can?! Well, here I am again, baking a cake in the shape of a doughnut! This chocolate cake recipe is one of the easiest you'll find and a bundt tin makes any cake look impressive – just make sure you prepare the tin well! The icing is glossy, the cake is chocolatey and moist; basically you need to make this cake and no, you don't need a reason to. Just do it (it is a great celebration cake though!).

1 Preheat your oven to 160°C fan / 180°C / 350°F. Grease a 22cm (8½in) bundt tin with softened butter, and dust over a mixture of flour and cocoa powder (or use cake-release spray).

2 In a large bowl, cream together the butter and sugar until light and fluffy. Add the rest of your ingredients except the chocolate chips and mix using an electric hand mixer, to combine. Fold in your chocolate chips.

3 Spoon the mixture into the prepared tin and bake for 40-50 minutes, or until a skewer inserted comes out clean. Leave for 10 minutes in the tin before inverting onto a wire rack to cool completely.

4 To make the icing, melt together the butter and chocolate in a medium bowl. Gradually add the icing sugar. It will become quite thick. Gradually mix in enough boiling water for the icing to turn glossy, and a thick, pourable consistency.

5 Spoon the icing over the cake so it gently drips down the sides – it shouldn't be so runny that it completely drips off. Sprinkle with colourful sprinkles and enjoy.

TIP If you don't have a bundt tin, no worries: this cake is amazing as a loaf cake, just reduce the eggs to 3 and scale down the other ingredients accordingly (simply use a calculator to multiply each ingredient quantity by 0.6 to get the right amount). Bake for 50 minutes in a 900g (2lb) loaf tin (pan).

use dairy-free milk

 use lactose-free milk

 use lactose-free milk

 use dairy-free milk and use 3 tbsp aquafaba (whisked until frothy) instead of the egg

---

- 100g (½ cup minus 1 tbsp) butter, melted and cooled, plus extra for greasing
- 200g (1½ cups) gluten-free plain (all-purpose) flour
- 2 tsp gluten-free baking powder
- ½ tsp ground cinnamon
- 55g (¾ cup) soft dark brown sugar
- 120ml (½ cup) whole milk
- 1 large egg, beaten
- 2 tbsp golden syrup

For the sauce

- 150g (¾ cup) soft dark brown sugar
- 1½ tbsp cornflour (cornstarch)
- 500ml (2 cups) boiling water
- 1 tsp vanilla extract
- 1 tbsp golden syrup

SELF-SAUCING BUTTERSCOTCH PUDDING

Serves 7-8 ❀

Prep 15 mins **+ Cook** 40 mins

This recipe is in the book for my mum. At the time of writing, she has not yet tried my butterscotch pudding, but butterscotch has always been her favourite flavour! Butterscotch Angel Delight, anyone?! It was such a treat when we were growing up! Anyway, Mum, if you read this I promise to make this for you soon, and for anyone else, please do give this a try, and never fear the amount of water you put on top, it creates the best secret sauce later on!

1 Preheat your oven to 160°C fan / 180°C / 350°F. Butter a 18 x 28cm (7 x 11in) baking tin (pan).

2 In a bowl, mix together the flour, baking powder, cinnamon and sugar until well combined. Add the melted butter, milk, egg and golden syrup and mix once more until you have a thick batter. Spoon evenly into your prepared tin.

3 For the sauce, mix the sugar with the cornflour until really well combined. Sprinkle it over the top of the cake in a nice, thick layer.

4 Mix together the boiling water, vanilla extract and golden syrup then carefully pour it over the top.

5 Bake in the oven for 35–40 minutes until the sponge top is cooked. Leave to cool briefly before serving up. There should be a lovely butterscotch sauce beneath the sponge pudding top.

use dairy-free butter

 use dairy-free butter

- 200g (1 cup) caster (superfine) sugar
- 175g (1⅓ cups) gluten-free plain (all-purpose) flour
- 1 tsp gluten-free baking powder
- ¼ tsp xanthan gum
- 185g (¾ cup plus 1 tbsp) butter, melted

For the fruit layer

- 750g (1lb 10oz) berries (frozen or fresh) – I used frozen blueberries, blackberries and raspberries
- 70g (⅓ cup) caster (superfine) sugar
- 2½ tbsp cornflour (cornstarch)

VERY BERRY DUMP CAKE

Serves 6–8 ❄

Prep 10 mins **+** **Cook** 45 mins

If you raised an eyebrow at the name of this pud, then that means you automatically have no choice but to try it! It gets its name from how outrageously easy it is: you quite literally dump the ingredients on top of each other in a dish and bake it. What comes out is almost like a fruit cobbler with a crisp, golden top and sticky, juicy fruit beneath. If you're feeling lazy, this is most definitely the one for you.

1 Preheat your oven to 160°C fan / 180°C / 350°F.

2 Place your fresh or frozen fruit in the bottom of a 23 x 33cm (9 x 13in) baking tin (pan). Add the sugar and cornflour and mix it into the berries.

3 In a bowl, mix together the sugar, flour, baking powder and xanthan gum. Sprinkle this over the top of the fruit.

4 Pour the melted butter over the top; it doesn't matter if it's not all covered.

5 Bake for 45 minutes for fresh fruit or a little longer if using frozen, until the top has lots of golden patches.

6 Serve hot, with vanilla ice cream.

TIP You can use canned pie filling if you prefer, instead of the fruit, sugar and cornflour layer. You can also use any fruit that you like, fresh or frozen.

use dairy-free butter

 use dairy-free butter and use 6 tbsp aquafaba (whisked until frothy) instead of the eggs

---

- 250g (9oz) pitted dates, chopped
- 150ml (⅝ cup) boiling water
- 90g (⅓ cup plus 1 tbsp) butter
- 1 tsp bicarbonate of soda (baking soda)
- 100g (½ cup) light brown sugar
- 85g (3oz) walnuts, chopped, plus an extra 15g (½oz), chopped, for on top
- 2 medium eggs, beaten
- 225g (1¾ cups) gluten-free self-raising (self-rising) flour
- ¼ tsp xanthan gum
- ½ tsp gluten-free baking powder

DATE AND WALNUT LOAF

Serves 8 ❄

Prep 15 mins **+ Cook** 30 mins

The inspiration for this recipe? You guys requested it so many times that I had no choice! And I'm so glad you did because this humble classic quickly became one of my favourite bakes, with a wonderful fruity, almost caramel-like flavour packed into every slice. Serving suggestion: add a good slathering of butter to a slice and enjoy with a hot cuppa.

1 Preheat your oven to 150°C fan / 170°C / 340°F. Line a 900g (2lb) loaf tin (pan) with non-stick baking parchment.

2 Place the chopped dates, boiling water, butter, bicarb and sugar in a large bowl and mix together so the butter melts. Leave for about 15 minutes so that the mixture cools down a little.

3 Add the chopped walnuts and beaten eggs and mix again before adding the flour, xanthan gum and baking powder, mixing to combine.

4 Pour the mixture into the prepared tin, sprinkle with extra chopped walnuts and bake for about 60-65 minutes, covering loosely with foil if it starts to brown a little too much during cooking.

5 Allow to cool in the tin for a while before transferring to a wire rack to cool completely. Slice and enjoy as it is, or spread with a little butter.

use dairy-free butter, cream and milk

 use lactose-free milk and cream

 use lactose-free milk and cream

 use dairy-free butter, cream and milk, and use 9 tbsp aquafaba (whisked until frothy) instead of the egg

---

- 70g (½ cup) butter, softened, plus extra for greasing
- 10 slices of gluten-free bread
- 3 medium eggs
- 225ml (scant 1 cup) double (heavy) cream
- 225ml (scant 1 cup) whole milk
- 75g (6 tbsp) light brown sugar
- 1 tbsp maple syrup, plus extra to finish
- 40g (1½oz) pecan nuts, chopped, plus extra, toasted, to finish

For the topping
- 20g (1½ tbsp) butter, melted
- 2 tbsp maple syrup

MAPLE PECAN BREAD AND BUTTER PUDDING

Serves 6-8 ❄

Prep 10 mins **+ Cook** 30 mins

Maple pecan is my favourite flavour combination so I decided to try and put that together with one of my favourite desserts – bread and butter pudding. You'd think anything with bread in the name would be a big no for gluten-free folk; however, you would be wrong. I find being the only gluten-free bread eater in the house that I often have plenty left over, and what better way to use bread up than in a bread and butter pudding – it's comfort food at its very best!

1 Preheat your oven to 160°C fan / 180°C / 350°F. Lightly butter a 18 x 28cm (7 x 11in) ovenproof dish.

2 Lightly butter one side of each slice of bread then cut each into triangle quarters.

3 In a large bowl, mix the eggs, cream, milk, sugar, maple syrup and chopped pecan nuts.

4 Pop your sliced and buttered bread into the mixture and mix around so it's well coated. Leave for a couple of minutes to soak.

5 Spoon or pour your soaked bread and custard mixture into the buttered dish. You can do this neatly or not! Don't worry if any of the bread has broken up either.

6 Mix together the melted butter and maple syrup for the topping and drizzle this over the top of the pudding, then bake for about 30 minutes until the top is slightly crisp and the custard beneath is set.

7 Remove from the oven and top with a little extra maple syrup, and some toasted pecan nuts. Serve hot or cold, with cream or custard.

TIP Add a mashed banana or two to the custard mixture for an extra flavour dimension – it's great! You might need more or fewer slices of gluten-free bread depending on the size of your loaf... gluten-free bread can sometimes be very small!

use dairy-free butter and milk

 use lactose-free milk

 use dairy-free butter and milk, and use 3 tbsp aquafaba (whisked until frothy) instead of the egg

---

- 100g (1 cup) gluten-free oats
- 200g (¾ cup plus 2 tbsp) butter
- 70g (⅓ cup) light brown sugar
- 185g (6½oz) golden syrup
- 100g (3½oz) black treacle (molasses)
- 250g (2 cups) gluten-free self-raising (self-rising) flour
- 3–4 tsp ground ginger
- ¼ tsp xanthan gum
- 1 large egg, beaten
- 60ml (¼ cup) milk

YORKSHIRE PARKIN

Makes 12-16 slices ❅

Prep 15 mins **+ Cook** 1 hour

My first experience of eating parkin was when Mark and I used to live in Manchester. On a very chilly Saturday afternoon we visited Stockport market and I found somebody who was selling gluten-free parkin - result! This one is nice and fiery just like I remember it and, unlike with most baking, the longer you leave this one the better it gets (within reason of course!!).

1 Preheat your oven to 140°C fan / 160°C / 325°F. Line a 23cm (9in) square baking tin (pan) with non-stick baking parchment.

2 Blitz the oats in a food processor so they are fairly fine (but not complete dust).

3 Put the butter, sugar, golden syrup and black treacle into a small saucepan and heat until all melted together.

4 Combine the blitzed oats, flour, ginger and xanthan gum in a large bowl then add the melted butter and sugar mixture to it and mix. Stir in the egg and milk until combined.

5 Pour into your tin and bake in the oven for 50-60 minutes until a skewer comes out clean.

6 Allow to cool in the tin, then remove and cut into slices. Parkin is best after a few days, so wrap it up in some baking parchment and enjoy a few days later for the best flavour. I can never wait, though, and just enjoy it straight away – I know that's not what you're meant to do!

7 Again, not conventional, but I love it served warm with custard.

use dairy free butter

 swap the cherries for a handful of raspberries

- 50g (3½ tbsp) butter, softened
- 50g (¼ cup) light brown sugar
- 5-6 canned pineapple rings in syrup, drained
- Handful of glacé cherries

For the cake

- 100g (½ cup) golden caster (superfine) sugar
- 100g (½ cup minus 1 tbsp) butter
- 100g (¾ cup) gluten-free self-raising (self-rising) flour
- 1 tsp gluten-free baking powder
- 1 tsp vanilla extract
- 2 medium eggs
- 1 tbsp maple syrup or 1 tbsp syrup from the pineapple tin

PINEAPPLE UPSIDE DOWN CAKE

Serves 6-8 ❄

Prep 15 mins **+ Cook** 35 mins

As you might have seen from some of my other upside down cake recipes, I love to mix them up and use different fruits and flavours (which you can certainly do with this recipe too), but nothing quite beats the classic pineapple version. I've never spoken to anyone about this cake who hasn't called it retro, so yes, it is pretty retro, maybe a bit before my time, even; but let's bring it back!

1 Preheat your oven to 160°C fan / 180°C / 350°F.

2 In a medium bowl, cream together the softened butter and sugar, either with an electric hand mixer or by hand. Spread the mixture over the base and slightly up the sides of a round 20cm (8in) cake tin (pan).

3 Arrange the pineapple rings on top. If you have gaps you can cut up some of the rings to fit. Place glacé cherries in the rings, and extra dotted around if you wish.

4 Place all the cake ingredients in a bowl and mix using an electric whisk until light and fluffy. Spoon the mixture evenly into the tin, on top of the pineapple rings, and bake in the oven for about 35 minutes.

5 Remove from the oven and leave to cool slightly before turning out onto a plate.

use dairy-free butter, milk and chocolate

 use lactose-free milk and chocolate

 use lactose-free milk and chocolate

- 90g (⅓ cup plus 1 tbsp) butter, melted, plus extra for greasing
- 175g (1⅓ cups) gluten-free self-raising (self-rising) flour
- 1 tsp gluten-free baking powder
- 30g (1oz) unsweetened cocoa powder
- 200g (1 cup) caster (superfine) sugar
- Grated zest of 1–2 oranges
- 2 medium eggs
- 215ml (1 cup minus 1½ tbsp) milk
- 1 tsp orange extract
- 75g (2½oz) chocolate chips

For the topping

- 185g (1 cup minus 1 tbsp) light brown sugar
- 20g (¾ oz) unsweetened cocoa powder
- 1 tsp orange extract
- 600ml (2½ cups) boiling water

SLOW COOKER CHOCOLATE ORANGE FUDGE PUD

Serves 8

Prep 10 mins **+ Cook** 2 hours

Over the past couple of years I've really got into using my slow cooker. I used to think all you could do in it was a stew – how wrong was I?! You really can create some amazing sweet dishes in it, and the one dessert I always go back to is my chocolate orange fudge pudding. It creates a divine sauce beneath the sponge and takes minimal prep. Do remember that all slow cookers are slightly different, so check on your pud to ensure you don't overdo it – mine is a 6.5 litre (14 pint) one, so if yours is smaller you might need to reduce the quantities to fit and adjust the cooking time.

1 Grease the slow cooker dish with butter or a cooking spray.

2 In a large bowl, mix together the flour, baking powder, cocoa powder, caster sugar and orange zest.

3 In a separate bowl mix together the eggs, milk, melted butter and orange extract, then add to the dry ingredients. Mix thoroughly to ensure there are no lumps of flour, and it's well combined. Fold through the chocolate chips and pour the mixture into the prepared slow cooker dish.

4 For the topping, mix together the light brown sugar and cocoa powder and sprinkle this over the top of the cake batter. Mix the orange extract with the boiling water and carefully pour over the batter.

5 Cook on high for around 2 hours, checking after 1½ hours. Depending on your slow cooker, it might take up to 2½ hours. You are looking for a firm sponge top and middle but with a degree of moisture still beneath, as this is what forms your delicious chocolate sauce.

6 Serve warm with lots of the chocolate sauce over the top of it. I like mine with vanilla ice cream, but Mark likes his with chocolate custard.

To bake in the oven

Preheat your oven to 160°C fan / 180°C / 350°F and grease a 23 x 30cm (9 x 12in) dish with butter. Follow the method above but bake in the oven for about 40 minutes. Cover with foil if it browns too quickly.

use a hard dairy-free butter

 use a hard dairy-free butter

- 450-650g (1lb-1lb 7oz) cooking apples, peeled and chopped
- 40-60g (3-5 tbsp) light brown sugar
- ¼ tsp ground cinnamon

For the crumble

- 110g (scant ½ cup) cold butter, cubed
- 220g (1¾ cups) gluten-free plain (all-purpose) flour
- 90g (scant ½ cup) light brown sugar
- 1 tbsp ground cinnamon
- 50g (½ cup) gluten-free oats (optional)

EASY APPLE CRUMBLE

Serves 6-8 ❄

Prep 15 mins **+ Cook** 40 mins

I cannot believe we have got to my fourth book (ahh, still cannot believe I am writing that!) without me sharing my most classic of apple crumble recipes with you. I honestly am so sorry! Apple crumble is the queen of puddings (yes I know there is a dessert called 'Queen of Puddings' but it ain't got nothing on apple crumble!). Mum and I used to make this together a lot when I was young and it's pretty much the same, although I do add cinnamon to mine, which Mum doesn't do as she isn't a fan – sorry Mum!

1 Preheat your oven to 180°C fan / 200°C / 400°F.

2 For the crumble, rub the cold butter into the flour in a large mixing bowl, using your fingertips, until it resembles breadcrumbs. Or do this in a food processor, which is faster.

3 Mix in the sugar, cinnamon and oats, if using, and put to one side.

4 Place the chopped apples into a 23 x 30cm (9 x 12in) oven dish, sprinkle over the sugar and cinnamon and mix in so the chopped apples are coated. Evenly spoon your crumble mixture all over the top and pop in the oven for about 40 minutes until the fruit is cooked and the crumble is golden.

5 Serve hot or cold, with custard or ice cream.

TIP This crumble is perfect for switching the fruit, depending on what you have. Some of the combinations I like include: half apple, half rhubarb; half apple, half pear; half apple, half plum; apple and a mix of berries.

- 200g (7oz) gluten-free digestive biscuits (graham crackers)
- 1 tbsp unsweetened cocoa powder
- 80g (⅓ cup plus 1 tsp) butter
- 150g (5oz) milk chocolate
- 240g (8½oz) condensed milk
- 250g (9oz) dark (bittersweet) chocolate

For the mint filling
- 350g (2½ cups) icing (confectioners') sugar, sifted
- 30g (2 tbsp) butter, softened
- 1½ tsp peppermint extract
- 3½ tbsp boiling water
- Green food colouring gel, to taste

MINT SLICE

Makes 15 ❄

Prep 20 mins + **Chill** 45 mins

These mint slices combine all your favourite mint chocolate sweets, cookies and desserts into one. They're basically three layers of pure awesome. The base almost has a fudgy quality to it thanks to the condensed milk, the middle layer is refreshingly sweet and… green (if you have food colouring!). Plus, the dark chocolate top is the perfect contrast in texture with a lovely snap. You can always finish them off with some mint chocolates too, but I often find that they're perfect without!

1 Line a 23cm (9in) square baking tin (pan) with non-stick baking parchment, leaving enough overhang to help you lift it out later.

2 Blitz the digestive biscuits to crumbs in a food processor (or place in a zip-lock bag and bash with a rolling pin), then stir in the cocoa powder so it is evenly dispersed.

3 Place the butter, milk chocolate and condensed milk in a microwavable bowl and melt together in the microwave. Stir thoroughly, then add it to the crushed biscuits. Mix together to combine.

4 Press the mixture into your prepared tin and place in the fridge (or freezer) while you prepare the mint filling.

5 Place the icing sugar, soft butter, peppermint extract, boiling water and green food colouring (add until it's as green as you'd like it) in a bowl and mix together until smooth and a spreadable consistency.

6 Spread over the top of the base and pop in the fridge for 15 minutes.

7 Melt the dark chocolate and pour over the mint layer. Then allow to set in the fridge.

8 Lift out of the tin and carefully cut into slices or squares. If you've left it to get really hard, use a hot knife and carefully saw through so the chocolate doesn't crack and the mint layer doesn't push out the sides.

TIP Add some mint-flavoured chocolates to the top before the chocolate layer has set, for an extra minty kick!

use dairy-free butter, cream and chocolate

 use lactose-free chocolate and whipping cream

 use vegetarian marshmallows

 use dairy-free butter, cream, chocolate and vegan marshmallows

- 125g (½ cup plus 1 tbsp) butter, plus extra for greasing
- 200g (7oz) dark (bittersweet) chocolate
- 200g (7oz) milk chocolate
- 150g (5oz) golden syrup
- 175g (6oz) gluten-free biscuits, such as digestive (graham crackers), cookies and cream, etc.
- 100g (3½oz) mini marshmallows
- 100g (3½oz) dried fruit, such as raisins, cherries, etc.
- 100g (3½oz) chocolate bars, such as chocolate honeycomb, etc.

For the ganache

- 120ml (½ cup) double (heavy) cream
- 120g (4oz) chocolate, chopped
- Extra chocolates, to decorate

Pictured on page 211

DIY CHOCOLATE FRIDGE CAKE

Serves 10-12 ❄

Prep 20 mins + Chilling

If you like a customizable recipe, this is the one for you. While the base chocolate mixture stays constant you really can switch up the other elements; just make sure they add up to a similar weight to the recipe below. You can also switch up the tin you make this in, using whatever you've got to hand! I recently read that this is the Queen's favourite cake, and after one bite, you'll definitely know exactly why.

1 Grease a 20cm (8in) round, deep, loose-bottomed or springform tin (pan) with butter and line the base with non-stick baking parchment.

2 Melt the butter, chocolates and golden syrup together either in the microwave or in a bain-marie. Place in a large bowl once melted.

3 Break up the biscuits and remaining additions and add them all into the melted chocolate mixture. Ensure that all the things you add are well coated but there is still some melted chocolate liquid left too – this will help to fill any gaps.

4 Pour the mixture into the prepared tin and press it down firmly. Place in the fridge while you make the ganache topping.

5 Pour the cream into a small saucepan and place over a low heat until just before it begins to boil. Add your chopped chocolate to a heatproof bowl and pour the hot cream onto the chocolate. Mix together until smooth, then pour on top of your fridge cake. Place in the fridge to set fully.

6 Remove the cake from the fridge and carefully remove from the tin before decorating with any extra chocolates. Cut into slices to serve – always slice with a warm, sharp knife; this really helps to get a clean slice.

TIP Don't want to do a chocolate ganache top? Just top with melted chocolate and leave to set in the fridge. It will set even more quickly.

use dairy-free butter, chocolate and caramel

 use lactose-free chocolate and caramel

 use lactose-free chocolate and caramel

 use vegetarian marshmallows

 combine the dairy-free and veggie advice

- 200g (7oz) marshmallows
- 70g (⅓ cup) butter
- 100g (3½oz) caramel
- 180g (6oz) gluten-free puffed rice cereal
- 230g (8oz) milk chocolate
- 70g (2½oz) white chocolate
- 16–25 gluten-free pretzels (optional)

STICKY TOFFEE CRISPY SQUARES

Makes 9–16 ❄

Prep 15 mins **+ Chilling**

What do you get when you put one of my favourite desserts (sticky toffee pud) with one of my favourite chocolate bars I can no longer eat (Toffee Crisp)? You get my Sticky Toffee Crispy Squares, of course! The first time I tested these out Mark took round a batch to his parents and sister and they were gone within seconds, so I think that says it all.

1 Line a 23cm (9in) square baking tin (pan) with non-stick baking parchment.

2 Put the marshmallows and butter into a large saucepan and place over a low heat. Keep stirring until melted. Remove from the heat and stir in the caramel.

3 Put your puffed rice into a large mixing bowl and pour over the caramel marshmallow mixture. Mix it in so all the puffed rice is covered evenly.

4 Spoon the mixture into your prepared tin and press it down, then place in the fridge briefly.

5 Melt your milk and white chocolate in separate bowls in the microwave then pour the milk chocolate over the mixture, spreading it to the edges. Drizzle over the white chocolate and, using a skewer, swirl it around to make a pattern. Optionally add pretzels all over the top so when you cut it, each square has one.

6 Pop in the fridge to set. Once set, cut into squares and enjoy!

TIP You can remove the caramel to have classic rice krispie squares, or add 100g (3½oz) chocolate to the butter and marshmallows, and remove the caramel, to make chocolate ones.

use a hard dairy-free butter and cream cheese (minimum 23% fat), or make a dairy free buttercream frosting instead

 use lactose-free cream cheese (minimum 23% fat)

- 260g (9oz) overripe bananas, mashed
- 170g (¾ cup) butter, softened
- 170g (¾ cup plus 1½ tbsp) caster (superfine) sugar
- 3 large eggs
- 260g (2 cups) gluten-free self-raising (self-rising) flour
- ¾ tsp gluten-free baking powder
- ¼ tsp xanthan gum

For the cream cheese frosting

- 100g (scant ½ cup) butter, softened
- 100g (scant ¾ cup) icing (confectioners') sugar
- 200g (7oz) cream cheese
- 1 tsp vanilla extract

BANANA TRAYBAKE

Serves 9 ❄

Prep 15 mins **+ Cook** 35 mins

'This banana cake really tastes like banana!' This is what Mark said after his first mouthful. I laughed. 'Of course it does, it's a banana cake,' I said! I do get what he means, though, as the sponge is super-light yet certainly packs a banana punch. It really complements the tang of the cream cheese frosting perfectly. Oh, and did I mention this is an all-in-one sponge too? Easy!

1 Preheat your oven to 160°C fan / 180°C / 350°F. Line a 23cm (9in) square baking tin (pan) with non-stick baking parchment.

2 Put all the cake ingredients into a large bowl and mix together until combined, light and fluffy (I use an electric hand mixer for this). Spoon the mixture into your prepared tin.

3 Bake in the oven for 35 minutes until golden and cooked through. Allow to cool in the tin for 15 minutes or so until firm enough to carefully lift out of the tin and fully cool on a wire rack.

4 For the cream cheese frosting, place the butter in a large bowl and mix for about 3 minutes using an electric hand mixer until it has turned a lot paler. Add your icing sugar and mix for a further 3 minutes.

5 Before you add the cream cheese, ensure that there is no excess liquid in the tub (if buying in a tub) – simply drain it if needed. Add to the bowl with the vanilla extract and mix for 2 more minutes until well combined and the icing is light and fluffy, without lumps.

6 Spread over the cooled banana sponge and then slice into squares.

TIP If freezing, add the frosting once defrosted. Use light brown sugar in the sponge and drizzle with caramel at the end to make a banoffee traybake instead of just banana!

GLUTEN-FREE SELF-RAISING (SELF-RISING) FLOUR

Makes 1kg (7½ cups)

Prep 2 mins

- 500g (3¾ cups) gluten-free plain (all-purpose) flour
- 6 tsp gluten-free baking powder
- 1 tsp xanthan gum

Gluten-free self-raising flour is readily available across all supermarkets in the UK. But if you can't find it where you live, you can easily make your own using the ratios below.

1 Simply combine all the ingredients in a large mixing bowl and mix thoroughly, then store in a large airtight container. Consider labelling it so you can tell it apart from other flour.

2 Use whenever a recipe calls for gluten-free self-raising flour.

GLUTEN-FREE PLAIN (ALL-PURPOSE) FLOUR

Makes 1kg (7½ cups)

Prep 2 mins

- 500g (3 cups) rice flour
- 150g (1 cup) tapioca starch
- 150g (¾ cup) potato starch
- 150g (1¼ cups) cornflour (cornstarch)
- 50g (scant ½ cup) buckwheat flour

If you live in the UK, you can easily find gluten-free plain (all-purpose) flour in supermarkets; in which case, you don't need this recipe! This recipe is for anyone who can't easily source gluten-free plain flour where they live or for anyone who has had mixed results using their country's equivalent. As commercial blends contain flours/starches in specific quantities, they can vary wildly depending on where you live in the world – and so can your baking results. So here's a blend you can rely on for using in this book – you can easily purchase these starches and flours online.

1 Simply combine all the ingredients in a large mixing bowl and mix thoroughly, then store in a large airtight container. Consider labelling it so you can tell it apart from other flour!

2 Use whenever a recipe calls for gluten-free plain flour.

TIP Ensure all the flours and starches that you use for the blend do not have 'may contain' warnings for gluten. I find this is especially relevant when sourcing tapioca starch and buckwheat flour.

EGG CONVERSION GUIDE

Did you know that a large egg in the UK is actually bigger than in the USA, Canada and Australia? Me neither! That's why I thought I'd pop in a handy egg conversion guide in the back of this book to help make things simple.

That way, when a recipe calls for a small, medium or large egg, you can use the table below to work out exactly what that means for you. I've used UK egg sizes in all my recipes, so just convert from there.

	UK	USA	Canada	Australia
Small	53g and under	42.5g / 1½oz	42g / 1½oz	N/A
Medium	53-63g	49.6g / 1¾oz	49g / 1¾oz	43g
Large	63-73g	56.7g / 2oz	56g / 2oz	52g
Extra large	73g and over	63.8g / 2¼oz	63g / 2¼oz	60g
Jumbo	N/A	70.9g / 2½oz	70g / 2½oz	68g

And just in case you're too lazy to look at anything presented in a table (like I am), here's your cheat sheet! Maybe we can call a meeting of all our world leaders and agree on a uniform egg size in future?

So when a recipe in this book calls for a **small egg**, you should use a:

USA: medium egg
Canada: medium egg
Australia: large egg

When a recipe in this book calls for a **medium egg**, you should use a:

USA: large egg
Canada: large egg
Australia: extra-large egg

When a recipe in this book calls for a **large egg**, you should use a:

USA: extra-large egg
Canada: extra-large egg.
Australia: jumbo egg

GAS MARK CONVERSION GUIDE

Here's a helpful table for oven temperature conversions depending on the kind of oven you use.

Celsius (fan)	Celsius	Fahrenheit	Gas mark
100	120	250	½
120	140	285	1
130	150	300	2
140	160	325	3
160	180	350	4
170	190	375	5
180	200	400	6
200	220	425	7
210	230	450	8
230	250	480	9
240	260	500	10

INDEX

ACKNOWLEDGEMENTS

Though I'm the author of this book, without these awesome humans, this book physically wouldn't exist. So that deserves a round of applause, don't you think?

Firstly, thank you to the 'Quad Squad' at Quadrille for all the behind-the-scenes know-how that not only went into bringing this book to life, but also putting it on shelves across the globe. I feel so lucky I get to work with you all.

I want to personally thank Sarah Lavelle for her unwavering faith in me and for always helping me to make the lives of gluten-free people easier, one book at a time.

Thank you to my super-star editor, Harriet Webster, for overseeing this book with care from start to finish (and for putting up with my endless edits). Needless to say, I appreciate the *huge* help in curating all the awesome things I'm wearing throughout this book.

Thanks again to my copy editor, Sally Somers, for being brave enough to be one of the first people to read my drafts; always emerging with valuable insight and advice.

A big high five to designer, Emily Lapworth, for waving her magic wand of awesomeness over the pages of this book once again – it's vibrant, inviting and so incredibly readable, which is more than I could have ever asked for.

Thank you to Hannah Hughes for all the truly mind-blowing food photography (we'd expect no less). I'm so happy with how all the photos of me turned out... especially when I often feel like a deer in headlights in front of the camera!

Thank you to Emily Kydd and Susanna Unsworth for their flawless food-styling, which never ceases to amaze me; if I could safely eat the actual pages of this book, I probably would. Thanks to Rebecca Newport for the carefully curated prop styling, which never fails to seamlessly slot into the aesthetic of this book.

Thank you to Cat Parnell for her hair and make-up magic on set – now all I need is for you to teach me how to do it myself for the other 360 days of the year! Thanks to Nicky for once again going out of her way to cut and colour my hair for this book (it looks amazing!) and thank you to Amy for your amazing nail art skills always.

Thanks to 'Team Laura' (Laura Willis and Laura Eldridge) and the Publicity Team for flying the flag for all of my books – it's been so amazing to see my recipes pop up in places I'd never expect in a million years.

Thanks to my 3-in-1 boyfriend, recipe tester and proofreader, Mark, for putting in so much time, care and thought into this book without a second thought. Thanks to my dog and mini mascot, Peggy, who either loves keeping me company when I'm creating recipes, or is only there because I sometimes give her a piece of raw carrot.

Thank you to my Mum and Dad for always supporting me in more ways than I can even count – I hope I've done you proud!

Thanks again to my brother Charlie, Gemma and the Farrow clan, as well as Mark's mum, dad and sister, Lisa, for all the constant support and positivity.

And finally, thanks a million to all my dedicated followers and readers for the constant love and support across all of my books so far. I hope you all know how much I appreciate it and the extent to which our online chats influence everything I do. So, if there's any way I can help to make your gluten-free life easier, please don't hesitate to let me know!

Managing Director
Sarah Lavelle

Commissioning Editor
Harriet Webster

Copy Editor
Sally Somers

Art Direction and Design
Emily Lapworth

Designer
Alicia House

Photographer
Hannah Hughes

Food Stylist
Emily Kydd

Prop Stylist
Rebecca Newport

Make-up Artist
Cat Parnell

Head of Production
Stephen Lang

Production Controller
Sabeena Atchia

First published in 2022 by Quadrille,
an imprint of Hardie Grant Publishing

Quadrille
52–54 Southwark Street
London SE1 1UN
quadrille.com

Text © Becky Excell 2022
Photography © Hannah Hughes 2022
Design and layout © Quadrille 2022

Cataloguing in Publication Data:
a catalogue record for this book
is available from the British Library.

UK ISBN: 978 1 78713 962 6
US + AUS ISBN: 978 1 78713 825 4

Printed in China

MIX
Paper from
responsible sources
FSC™ C020056

FSC
www.fsc.org

This book is not intended
as a substitute for genuine medical
advice. The reader should consult
a medical professional in matters relating
to their health, particularly with regard
to symptoms of IBS and coeliac disease.

FODMAP information was correct at
the time of writing, but please check the
Monash University FODMAP app for
the latest information on serving sizes.
These may change via updates
in the future.

Also available:

How to Make Anything Gluten Free

How to Bake Anything Gluten Free

How to Plan Anything Gluten Free

Available online and in all good bookshops